LETTERS TO A NEW BELIEVER

For Joshua
with love from Great-Uncle *[signature]*
12/09

You may find these letters useful to you in a few
years time / so hold on to them!

For Ian

Letters To A
New Believer

David J. Newell

JOHN RITCHIE LTD
CHRISTIAN PUBLICATIONS

40 Beansburn, Kilmarnock, Scotland

ISBN-13: 978 1 904064 64 0
ISBN-10: 1 904064 64 7

Copyright © 2008 by John Ritchie Ltd.
40 Beansburn, Kilmarnock, Scotland

www.ritchiechristianmedia.co.uk

Typeset by John Ritchie Ltd., Kilmarnock
Printed by Bell & Bain Ltd., Glasgow

Contents

Letter No. 1:

Assurance

Thank you so very much for your surprise letter, delivered by hand on Saturday. It was such a delight to see you. It is a long time since I have read any correspondence that has so much cheered my heart. It has been my desire all through our friendship that you would one day come into the good of God's great salvation in Christ Jesus, and now, by His sovereign grace alone, you have. How glad I am to know that your sins are forgiven and that you have true "peace with God through our Lord Jesus Christ" (Rom 5.1)! This means that, were you to die right now, you would pass immediately into the presence of your Lord. As Paul says: "Therefore *we are* always confident, knowing that, whilst we are at home in the body, we are absent from the Lord: (For we walk by faith, not by sight:) We are confident, *I say*, and willing rather to be absent from the body, and to be present [at home] with the Lord" (2 Cor 5.6-8). Never forget to spend time praising God for His great kindness to you.

I realise that you will find it hard at times to grasp the fact that you are now really and eternally saved – but do not worry, as this is a common experience. Our confidence must rest in God's word alone, not in feelings (which come and go with the weather), nor in the assurances of mere humans (who can be wrong). When Paul wrote to the Thessalonian believers he rejoiced that their faith was not in men's opinions but in God's word:

> "For this cause also thank we God without ceasing, because, when ye received the word of God which ye heard of us, ye received *it* not *as* the word of men, but as it is in truth, the word of God, which effectually worketh also in you that believe" (1 Thess 2.13).

9

If my faith depends on the clever arguments or rhetorical powers of a man then it will always be vulnerable to the cleverer arguments and superior oratory of another. But we rest in God. The Bible says that "faith cometh by hearing, and hearing by the word of God" (Rom 10.17) – a key verse about faith. Your letter speaks of how much faith it takes to be saved. It is neither the quality nor the quantity of your faith that saves – it is *Christ* who saves wretched sinners like you and me. You can always pray like the poor father in the gospel, "Lord, I believe – help Thou my unbelief" (Mark 9.24). My faith is simply a feeble hand that stretches out to lay hold of God's freely-provided gift (Rom 6.23). Consider: two men place their money in a bank for safe-keeping. One has implicit confidence in the bank's financial probity and sleeps easy at night. The other is racked with anxieties and doubts, fearful lest he lose all his assets. But the bank is completely sound. Which man is more secure? In fact, *both are equally safe* – but only one knows it and lives in the enjoyment of it. You see, when the Lord Jesus Christ died on the cross for sinners like us, He cried out in triumph, "It is finished" (John 19.30). This means (i) that His death was the sufficient payment for our sins, (ii) that the work of salvation was complete and done, (iii) that there is nothing more for me to do. No wonder Paul can write,

> "For the which cause I also suffer these things: nevertheless I am not ashamed: for I know whom I have believed, and am persuaded that he is able to keep that which I have committed unto him against that day" (2 Tim 1.12).

By the way, I hope you are looking these verses up! Never take my word for it: always check the Bible. You *are* safe right now; but feed on the word of God and you will become more and more *certain*. Please read through the enclosed booklet *Safety, Certainty and Enjoyment*, which has been much used of God over the years to bring Christians into true peace of soul.

When doubts come into your mind (and they will because Satan does his best to make believers doubt their salvation) simply run to the word (Proverbs 18.10) and get it into your heart. When Bunyan's Christian was incarcerated in Doubting Castle he began to lose his assurance. But the remedy was to remember that he had a key on his person called Promise (meaning the promises of God's word). Try the following promises for your own encouragement:

- John 5.24 (which we read yesterday)

- John 3.16 (God loved and gave – you have believed, and therefore you *have right now* eternal life and will never perish)
- Romans 10.9-10 (you have confessed Jesus as Lord and have believed in your heart that God raised Him from the dead – one of the great evidences that His death has been fully accepted by God as the payment for your sins – therefore you *are* saved).
- John 6.37 (the first half of this verse relates to God's amazing purpose from eternity past, but the second half relates to our coming to the Saviour – note His promise. You say in your letter that you have a sense of God's work in your salvation – I can guarantee that as you grow you will realise more and more that, as Jonah learnt in an unusual academy, "salvation is of the Lord" (Jonah 2.9)
- Matthew 11.28-29 (you have come, so the Lord Jesus has guaranteed to "give you rest")
- Acts 2.21 (everyone who calls on the name of the Lord, cries to Him for deliverance, "shall be saved")

May you learn to rest on God's infallible word as the rock-solid foundation for your faith. Feed on it daily, read, read, read it for your very life, and let it get down into your soul to influence your conduct in this world.

I said yesterday that, since you have now been born again by the power of God (see John 1.12-13; John 3.3-7), you have just entered into new life and, like a new-born child, you have four basic requirements: FOOD (the Bible), BREATH (prayer), WARMTH (fellowship with other believers in a biblical local church) and EXERCISE (telling others about your Saviour). Conversion is not the end but the beginning, the beginning of a wonderful new quality of life lived in a loving relationship with the God of heaven who has saved you that you might bring Him glory in this world (read Ephesians 1.1-14, and note especially the recurring phrase in verses 6,12,14). Is it not amazing that the Living God should wish to get glory from sinners like us?

But as usual I am going on far too long - please forgive me. I have placed a few booklets in this package which I hope you might find time to read. They are designed to direct you to the word for assurance and feed your new life with God's truth. You will now all the more be in my prayers – that you might be protected from temptation, kept safe in God's love, and that you might grow into a strong and stable believer in Christ.

Yours affectionately in Christ Jesus

Letter No 2:

The Three Tenses of Salvation

It was again a great delight to have you over on Saturday afternoon. Thanks for making the effort to call in – you know how much I enjoy your company.

I thought I'd just jot down the few things we spoke about so that you can check up the verses in your Bible. One of the things you will begin to do as you start to feed on God's word is to underline or highlight verses and passages which encourage your soul. Do not worry about marking a Bible– it is a valuable way to help one's study. As they say, a Bible that is falling to pieces usually belongs to someone who isn't! Salvation, you see, is a vast truth and goes way beyond what is probably our immediate concern at the moment of conversion - to be rescued from the eternal judgment of God against our sins. That is why the writer to the Hebrews calls it "so great salvation" (Heb 2.3).

It comprehends, **first**, a past tense. Every believer in Christ Jesus is permanently freed from the eternal penalty of his sins because the Saviour died in his place on Calvary. If God has poured out His anger against my sins upon His Son, then there can be no judgment awaiting me. As Paul says,

> "by grace <u>you have been saved</u> through faith. And this is not your own doing; it is the gift of God, not a result of works, so that no one may boast" (Eph 2.8-9).

And again,

> "God, <u>who saved us</u> and called us to a holy calling, not because of our works but because of his own purpose and

grace, which he gave us in Christ Jesus before the ages began" (2 Tim 1.9).

And again,

> "But when the goodness and loving kindness of God our Saviour appeared, he saved us, not because of works done by us in righteousness, but according to his own mercy, by the washing of regeneration and renewal of the Holy Spirit" (Titus 3.5).

Because *you have been saved* by God's free grace on the basis of the finished work of Christ, nothing can ever "separate you from the love of God in Christ Jesus our Lord" (Rom 8.39).

Second, salvation has a present tense in that the God who saved me from Hell is currently working in my life to deliver me daily from the power of indwelling sin. Remember the Saviour's earthly name: "thou shalt call his name JESUS: for he shall save his people [not simply from hell, but] from their sins" (Matt 1.21) The saved man must display a change of life. The Lord Jesus Christ died to rescue me from Hell, but He lives for evermore at God's right hand to keep and sustain me.

> "For if, when we were enemies, we were reconciled to God by the death of his Son, much more, being reconciled, we shall be saved [daily] by his life" (Rom 5.10).

> "For the word of the cross is folly to those who are perishing, but to us who are being saved it is the power of God" (1 Cor 1.18).

The power of God works on my behalf to maintain me day by day, to enable me to begin to live in a godless world in a way that glorifies Him. Christians call this **sanctification** (which means simply setting apart – that is, I am set apart from sin and the world for God's own pleasure and use). It is a daily reality brought about by reading, believing and obeying God's word (see John 17.17). As Paul says, "we beseech you, brethren, and exhort *you* by the Lord Jesus, that as ye have received of us how ye ought to walk and to please God, *so* ye would abound more and more. For ye know what commandments we gave you by the Lord Jesus. For this is the will of God, *even* your sanctification" (1 Thess 4.1-3). Yes, you have been saved from the eternal penalty of sin, but *you are right now being saved* from the power of sin. God aims to shape you so that you can bring Him delight.

Finally, there is the future tense of salvation (which we sometimes call **glorification**). My body is marred by sin and therefore mortal. When you get saved you do not immediately receive a super new body free from disease and death – after all, Christians die! Indeed, sickness and suffering are tools the Lord uses to educate His people in real godliness. But, when the Lord Jesus returns, we shall gain a body suited to our heavenly home, a body free from sin, decay and death (see 1 Cor 15.49-57). Therefore Paul exhorts believers:

> *"it is* high time to awake out of sleep: for <u>now *is* our salvation nearer</u> than when we believed" (Rom 13.11).
> "God hath not appointed us to wrath, but <u>to obtain salvation</u> by our Lord Jesus Christ" (1 Thess 5.9-10).
> "we ourselves groan within ourselves, <u>waiting for the adoption, *to wit,* the redemption of our body"</u> (Rom 8.23).

Belonging to the Lord Jesus Christ means we have everything to look forward to. Never forget that this great salvation cost the Lord Jesus the shedding of His blood to secure all these blessings for you. Keep thanking Him. You are in my thoughts and prayers. May the Lord uphold you daily and keep you for Himself.

Yours affectionately in Christ Jesus

Letter No 3:

The Names of Believers

I thought I'd continue these letters (since I seem to have got into the swing of them) and try to open up another great topic in relation to your new-found salvation in Christ Jesus. We have already touched on (i) how you can be assured of your salvation, and (ii) what salvation means. Every believer has been rescued from the penalty, is being delivered daily from the power, and will be finally snatched from the very presence of sin. Now let me draw your attention to what we are in the sight of God. When I was born physically I became instantaneously if unconsciously a son, a grandson, a brother, a nephew, a consumer. Similarly the believer in Christ enters a range of relationships at the moment of new birth. Most of the terms used to describe our position by grace turn up significantly in the Book of the Acts, the great history of the spread of the Christian gospel after the ascension of Christ.

First, we are **believers**:

> "And <u>believers</u> were the more added to the Lord, multitudes
> both of men and women" (Acts 5.14; 1 Tim 4.12)

This obviously places the emphasis upon what we did the moment we surrendered to the Lord Jesus Christ: we trusted Him, taking Him at His word. But faith is not confined to the past – it is the daily life of the soul, for "the just shall live by faith" (Rom 1.17). Yes, you believed in the Saviour at a point in time and immediately came into peace with God (Rom 5.1), but you keep on believing, growing daily in your knowledge of His greatness and glory.

Second, we are **disciples:**

"And the word of God increased; and the number of the <u>disciples</u> multiplied in Jerusalem greatly" (Acts 6.7; 9.1,19).

Disciples set themselves to learn about, follow and obey their Master (John 1.37). Disciples are marked by obedience to the Lord Jesus and His word (John 8.31). The related word in English is *discipline*, for discipleship is not easy – it demands a tough loyalty to the Saviour through thick and thin. The Lord spoke frankly about the cost in Luke 14.26-35.

Third, we are **brethren**. This reminds us that, being born into God's family, we instantly become related to all other genuine believers in Christ (Matt 23.8). The newly-saved Saul of Tarsus came into the good of this in Jerusalem, where the same people he had hitherto persecuted became his spiritual family, providing him with support and encouragement. Hearing of Jewish plots against his life:

> "When the <u>brethren</u> knew, they brought him down to Caesarea, and sent him forth to Tarsus" (Acts 9.30).

I think one of the most wonderful moments in Saul's experience as a believer was when Ananias called him "brother Saul" (Acts 9.17). Christians love one another because Christ first loved them in all their wretched sinfulness: "A new commandment I give unto you, That ye love one another; as I have loved you, that ye also love one another" (John 13.34). The model of this love is the Lord Jesus Himself – He loved us selflessly, constantly, sacrificially. That is why Christians put themselves out for one another (1 Peter 1.22).

Fourth, we are **saints**. This may seem strange, as so many people have the false idea that you have to be dead to be a saint. But the Bible makes it clear that if you are not one of the saints before you die, you never will be. Saint simply means someone who is set apart (the Greek words for holy, consecrate, sanctify and saint are all related).

> "Then Ananias answered, Lord, I have heard by many of this man, how much evil he hath done to thy <u>saints</u> at Jerusalem" (Acts 9.13,32,41).

Yes, you are now one of God's saints. By His grace, you are set apart for His delight, snatched from a hell-bent world, and given over to Him. But saints should live like saints. Paul begins a letter to the worst church in the New Testament by reminding them of what God has called them:

"Unto the church of God which is at Corinth, to them that are sanctified in Christ Jesus, called <u>saints,</u> with all that in every place call upon the name of Jesus Christ our Lord, both theirs and ours" (1 Cor 1.2). We have to pray for help to live a holy life for our holy God.

Fifth, we are **Christians**. It is a surprise to find how rarely this term appears in the Bible (only thrice), but it clearly underlines our indissoluble connection with the person of the Lord Jesus:

> "And the disciples were called <u>Christians</u> first in Antioch" (Acts 11.26).

Since we belong to Him we should live in a way that speaks well of Him. I imagine that those disciples were called Christians because they kept on referring to their Saviour by name (1 Pet 4.16).

Sixth, we are **children of God** by faith alone: "For ye are all the <u>children of God</u> by faith in Christ Jesus" (Gal 3.26). This emphasizes the privilege of being related to the Living God of the universe. By nature we were "children of wrath and sons of disobedience" (Eph 2.2-3) but God has radically changed our family relationship for ever. God's children should reflect something of the character of their Father.

Finally, we belong to a **holy priesthood**. In the Old Testament only one family from Israel was selected to be priests and represent the whole nation before God, but in the New Testament all believers in the Lord Jesus (male and female, old and young) are priests with the glorious responsibility of offering up worship to God:

> "Ye also, as lively stones, are built up a spiritual house, an <u>holy priesthood,</u> to offer up spiritual sacrifices, acceptable to God by Jesus Christ" (1 Pet 2.5; Heb 10.19-25).

Christianity does not divide between clergy and laity – rather it announces that *all* God's saved ones are equipped to serve Him. Our spiritual sacrifices consist of our praises (Heb 13.15), our possessions (Heb 13.16) and our persons (Rom 12.1-2). We are not only saved from hell, but privileged in this world to give God the worship which is His due.

You are in my thoughts and prayers. May the Lord teach you from His word and lead you in His paths of righteousness.

Yours affectionately in Christ Jesus

WEEK FOUR

Letter No 4:

Justification

Since you mentioned the subject of JUSTIFICATION the other day, I thought I'd try to outline a little of its significance. Being saved, you see, involves learning a new vocabulary to express all the great things that God does for His people the minute they place their confidence in His Beloved Son. As you grow to know the Bible better you will begin to understand the value and meaning of these technical terms. For example, every believer in Christ is *regenerated* by the Spirit of God, *reconciled* to God, *adopted* into God's family, *redeemed* from bondage to sin, and *sanctified* for God's pleasure.

First of all, let me define what justification means. It means to declare that someone is right or (if you prefer) not guilty. It is a judicial or court-room term, as when the judge says to the accused, "You are acquitted, and there remains no charge against you". This is illustrated in the Old Testament, where Jewish magistrates were instructed thus: "If there be a controversy between men, and they come unto judgment, that the judges may judge them; then they [the judges] shall justify the righteous, and condemn the wicked" (Deut 25.1) What the judge did made no essential difference to the man in the court: it simply formally announced him to be what he already was. The guilty man was condemned (declared guilty), and the righteous man was justified (declared to be right). What a judge must not do, of course, was "justify the wicked" (Exod 23.7). In fact, God specifically set His face against such injustice (Isa 5.20-23).

Trouble is, I am completely unrighteous before God because of my sinfulness. Paul's letter to the Romans makes that abundantly clear – we are all without excuse and utterly condemned. Whoever we are, the verdict is plain: "there is none righteous, no, not one...for all have sinned and come short of the glory of God" (Rom 3.10,23). The only thing I can expect from a holy God is condemnation and eternal judgment.

But here is the wonder of God's good news. The God who says "I will not justify the wicked" reveals Himself in the New Testament as One who justifies the ungodly (the wicked) (Romans 4.5)! How can this be? The answer is that what God's righteous law demands (the execution of the guilty) God's love has provided in the person of His Son who died in the place of guilty sinners like you and me. Because the full penalty of the broken law was meted out upon my sinless Substitute (the Lord Jesus Christ), God can pardon a sinner like me without in the least compromising His own righteous character. As Paul puts it, "to declare, I say, at this time his righteousness: that he [God] might be just, and the justifier of him which believeth in Jesus" (Rom 3.26). The most astonishing word in that verse is the simple connective "and". That God should be "just" is no surprise, for He is perfectly righteous in all He does – but that He should be just *and at the same time* able to declare guilty folk like you and me right (justified, acquitted, not guilty) in His sight is past understanding. It is because "the Lord hath laid on him [the Lord Jesus Christ] the iniquity of us all" (Isa 53.6). Justification is therefore that act of God whereby He declares the guilty but believing sinner righteous on the basis of the finished work of Christ on Calvary.

So how are we justified?

First, it is by God's **grace**: "being justified freely <u>by his grace</u> through the redemption that is in Christ Jesus" (Rom 3.24). That is to say, it is all a result of God's free kindness towards people who just do not deserve it. We cannot earn it, work for it, pay for it – every blessing comes to us on the basis of grace (unmerited favour).

Second, it is by **blood** (biblical shorthand for the death of Christ): "being now justified <u>by his blood,</u> we shall be saved from wrath through him" (Rom 5.9). I am justified because on the cross the Lord Jesus Christ endured the judgment my sins deserve.

Third, it is by **faith**: "being justified <u>by faith</u> we have peace with God" (Rom 5.1). It is only by faith in Christ Jesus that I can come into the good of justification – not through my works but through faith in *His* work.

Fourth, it is by **works**: "ye see then how that <u>by works</u> a man is justified, and not by faith only" (James 2.24). This does not contradict what has just been said, because if you read the context you will see that James is speaking about the kind of faith that results in a life of good works. Yes, it is faith alone that saves, but the faith that saves never comes alone. After all, the evidence that there has been a work of God in your soul is that you begin to live for God – faith may be invisible but it always shows on the outside of the believer.

Years ago Helen H. Shaw wrote a poem to sum it all up and I can do no better than quote it in full:

> God's sovereign grace selected me
> To have in heav'n a place;
> 'Twas the good pleasure of His will;
> I'm justified *by grace*.
>
> In due time Christ on Calv'ry died;
> There flowed that crimson flood
> Which makes the foulest white as snow;
> I'm justified *by blood*.
>
> God raised Him up – this is the pledge
> Should evil doubtings lour;
> His resurrection quells each fear;
> I'm justified *by power*.
>
> The Holy Spirit guided me
> To what the scripture saith.
> I grasped the truth: Christ died for me!
> I'm justified *by faith*.
>
> Now if you doubt that I am Christ's,
> If one suspicion lurks,
> I'll show by deed that I am His;
> I'm justified *by works*.
>
> I praise the Lord – 'tis all of Him
> The grace, the faith, the blood,
> The resurrection pow'r, the works;
> I'm justified *by God*!

Rejoice in your justification and keep going day by day. Feed on God's word and grow in grace.

Yours affectionately in Christ Jesus

WEEK FIVE

Letter No 5:

Redemption

I last wrote about the great subject of justification – one of the most important New Testament truths, as it guarantees so many blessings to the believer. All you have to do is read Romans 5.1-11 and look at Paul's list of the benefits of being justified: we have (right now) peace with God, access into a standing of grace before God, a joyful hope of God's glory in the future, and the ability to endure trials and afflictions in the present knowing that God uses all these for our ultimate good. Because we have been justified by faith we are at this very minute declared fit for God's presence. No wonder Paul concludes chapter 8 of his letter by saying that nothing can ever separate us from the love of God. But there are other technical terms to enjoy. For example, every believer in Christ has been **redeemed**.

Redemption means *deliverance from some form of bondage on the basis of the payment of a ransom price by a Redeemer*. Whereas justification finds me in the dock, a guilty sinner before God heading for eternal judgment, but declares me acquitted from all charges because another has suffered the penalty of the broken law in my place, redemption sees me in the slave market of sin, unable to free myself from bondage unless someone rescues me. There are therefore four ideas built into redemption: bondage, a redeemer, a price, and a deliverance.

The Bible clearly teaches that I am **ruined**, enslaved to sin and unable to do anything to set myself free. Listen to Paul: "Know ye not, that to whom ye yield yourselves servants to obey, his servants ye are to whom ye obey; whether of sin unto death, or of obedience unto righteousness? But God be thanked, that ye were the servants of sin, but ye have obeyed from the heart that form of doctrine which was delivered you. Being then made free from sin, ye became the servants of righteousness. I speak after the manner of men because of the infirmity of your flesh: for as ye have yielded your members servants to uncleanness and to iniquity unto iniquity; even so now yield your members servants to righteousness unto holiness. For when ye were the servants of sin, ye were free from righteousness" (Rom 6.16-20). The Lord Jesus sums it up crisply: "Verily, verily, I say unto you, Whosoever committeth sin is the servant [slave] of sin" (John 8.34). Despite all the celebrations over the abolition of the slave trade, the world is still full of slaves: people who think they are free to do as they like but who are actually trapped in sinful habits from which they cannot escape. Peter describes all the man-made liberation movements that have ever existed: "While they promise liberty, they themselves are the servants of corruption: for of whom a man is overcome, of the same is he brought in bondage" (2 Pet 2.19). Like the Israelites in Egypt, the sinner is trapped hopelessly in his misery: "and the children of Israel sighed by reason of the bondage, and they cried, and their cry came up unto God by reason of the bondage" (Exod 2.23).

Second, I need a **redeemer**: that is to say, because I am completely helpless ("dead in trespasses and sins") my only hope is in outside intervention. The whole concept of redemption was built into the family, social and national life of Old Testament Israel, so that God's people would be accustomed to its significance. For example, if you paid up to buy back the property of a relative who had fallen into debt you were a redeemer (Lev 25.23-25). But most important of all, every Israelite knew that he belonged to a nation redeemed by God Himself (Exod 6.6-8: Deut 7.6-8; 15.15). The annual Passover feast was a constant reminder of what Jehovah had done for His people (Exod 12.25-27). Now, all these Old Testament pictures of rescue point forward to what the Lord Jesus Christ did for us at Calvary. Just as Jehovah redeemed His people from terrible slavery when He brought them out of Egypt on the Passover night (Isa 43.1; Jer 50.33-34), so we have been rescued from the power and penalty of sin by the Lord Jesus Christ our Redeemer. He loved us and gave Himself for us (Gal 2.20).

Third, there has to be a **ransom price**. In Old Testament times, redemption always involved a cost. When the Israelites were liberated from Egypt a lamb had to be slain and its blood shed. Read carefully Exodus 12.1-13 and then see how the idea of the spotless Passover lamb is ultimately fulfilled in the Lord Jesus Christ:

> "The next day John seeth Jesus coming unto him, and saith,

Behold the Lamb of God, which taketh away the sin of the world" (John 1.29).

"Ye know that ye were not redeemed with corruptible things, *as* silver and gold, from your vain conversation *received* by tradition from your fathers; But with the precious blood of Christ, as of a lamb without blemish and without spot: Who verily was foreordained before the foundation of the world, but was manifest in these last times for you" (1 Pet 1.18-20).

We must never forget what it cost the Son of God to buy us for Himself, for He was our ransom price (Mark 10.45).

Fourth, there is the actual **rescue** and its consequences. Having been purchased by the Lord Jesus Christ I now belong to Him (1 Cor 6.19-20). Paul puts it memorably in Acts 27.23, when he speaks of "God, whose I am [the fact of redemption] and whom I serve [the proper response to redemption]". You see, God has bought me out from the slave market of sin to set me free – not to wander off alone but to serve Him for ever and ever. The Christian is free, not to continue in sin and self-will, but free to do what pleases God. To live in a loving relationship with the God who made us is the only true liberty (John 8.36; Gal 5.1). When the Israelites came out of Egypt God did not leave them to find their own way; rather, He guided them by a pillar of cloud so they would safely reach the land He had promised them (Exod 13.21-22; Isa 48.17). Redemption brings responsibilities. So too the New Testament lays down clear instructions for believers to follow today (Acts 2.41-42).

The best way to get this into your heart is to read the story of Israel's redemption as recorded in Exodus chapters 12 to 14. It is both a stunning historical account of God's power at work and a wonderful picture of what He has done for us through the Lord Jesus Christ. So do not forget; you belong to the Lord Jesus in a double way: first, He made you (John 1.3), and second He purchased you with His precious blood. What He said to Israel applies to us: "I have redeemed thee…thou art mine" (Isa 43.1-2). That is good reason to rejoice, to give thanks, and to live for Him who loved you.

Yours affectionately in Christ Jesus

WEEK SIX

Letter No 6:

Prayer

Another of those letters, I fear! At least you will have leisure to read this one now that your exams are all over. I trust that you will be able to spend some time simply relaxing and enjoying the rarity of Scottish sunshine.

Having written a little about key words of the Christian life (justification and redemption), I was tempted to launch straight into regeneration, reconciliation and sanctification, but you will be relieved to know that wiser counsels prevailed. I propose instead to talk a little about the spiritual exercise of prayer. *Exercise* may sound a strange word to use, but it highlights the fact that prayer is the believer's vital link with heaven, a spiritual activity essential to our growth in grace. George Herbert the poet, you will remember, calls it "God's breath in man returning to his birth". It is nowhere defined precisely in the Bible, but its contexts and its synonyms (see 1 Tim 2.1; Phil 4.6) indicate the meaning: prayer is simply speaking to God. After all, this is the way we get to know our friends down here – through opening up our hearts in conversation. And though God already knows every thought of our hearts (1 Kings 8.39; Psa 139.1-6) He loves His children to share them with Him.

It is also clear that prayer is as instinctive an activity of the child of God as is a baby's cry. The Lord Jesus gave instructions to His disciples on the subject prefaced by the remark "when [not *if*] ye pray" (Matt 6.5). The assumption is that the Lord's people pray. The new believers in Jerusalem "continued steadfastly in the apostles' doctrine and in fellowship and in the breaking of bread and in prayers" (Act 2.42). When the Lord instructed Ananias of Damascus to visit the recently saved Saul, the one piece of evidence He offered of the genuineness of Saul's conversion was this:

"Behold, he prayeth" (Acts 9.11). You see, before salvation we were completely out of touch with God (the mechanical recitation of prayers and religious ritual notwithstanding) because sinners are spiritually dead (Eph 2.1), "alienated from the life of God" (Eph 4.18). The respectable Pharisee Saul had never truly prayed before. Only as the Spirit of God makes us spiritually alive in Christ do we long to commune with our heavenly Father. This in itself is a wonderful token that we are really saved. See what Paul says in Romans 8:

> "For as many as are led by the Spirit of God, they are the sons of God. For ye have not received the spirit of bondage again to fear; but ye have received the Spirit of adoption, whereby we cry, Abba, Father. The Spirit himself beareth witness with our spirit, that we are the children of God" (Rom 8.14-16).

Further, there are different aspects of prayer. It involves for example, **adoration** (that is to say, praising God for all that He is in His greatness and glory). This is illustrated in Psalm 145. Go through that psalm and list all the things it tells us about God. Adoration is both proper, as God deserves our constant worship, and beneficial in that it lifts our minds up from ourselves and our trivial problems by engaging us with the greatest of all possible objects. We so often become self-preoccupied, which is a recipe for depression; to be taken up with God lifts the soul (Psa 103.1). Second, it includes **confession**: agreeing with God about our sins. Of course, when we first trusted Christ as Saviour we admitted our utter sinfulness and cast ourselves upon His mercy (Prov 28.13). But even after conversion we still have the "flesh" inside us (best understood by spelling it backwards and dropping the h = self), and need daily to confess our sins to receive God's gracious cleansing. "If we say that we have no sin, we deceive ourselves, and the truth is not in us. If we confess our sins, he is faithful and just to forgive us *our* sins, and to cleanse us from all unrighteousness" (1 John 1.8-9). Psalm 51 is a great example of confession, written after David became aware of the sins recorded in 2 Samuel 11. Third, there is **thanksgiving**, the essential ingredient of all prayer as we recognize our utter indebtedness to God's goodness (1 Thess 5.18). Our English "thank" is related etymologically to "think" – and truly, the more we think about what the Lord has done for us, the more we shall thank Him. Psalm 107 is an exhilarating model of thanksgiving. Fourth, there is **supplication** (making request). Being saved means we can approach God as Father and ask Him for what we need, knowing that He always has the best in store for His children:

"Ask, and it shall be given you; seek, and ye shall find; knock, and it shall be opened unto you: For every one that asketh receiveth; and he that seeketh findeth; and to him that knocketh it shall be opened . . . If ye then, being evil, know how to give good gifts unto your children, how much more shall your Father which is in heaven give good things to them that ask him?" (Matt 7.7-11).

We may well feel overawed and dumbstruck by this privilege, but the Holy Spirit Himself helps us in prayer (Rom 8.26).

Though prayer comprehends so many different elements, it need not be prolix. Sometimes all we can do is utter emergency prayers. The sinking Peter cried out "Lord save me!" (Matt 8.25; 14.30). God's children can approach Him anywhere, "to find grace to help in time of need" (Heb 4.16). When temptation strikes, pray! When you become especially aware of God's goodness to you, pray! And of course we should pray for one another: "praying always with all prayer and supplication in the Spirit, and watching thereunto with all perseverance and supplication for all saints" (Eph 6.18-19). One of the many benefits of local church fellowship is that it places us in a sphere where believers pray for each other.

Of course, to address the Living God of the universe requires fitting reverence. Yes, God is "our Father", but He is also "in heaven" and His name hallowed (Matt 6.9). Having spent most of our lives merely speaking to people like ourselves, it takes a while to adjust. The way to learn to pray is to get to know the word: we speak best to God after listening to what He has to say to us. Start the day with the scriptures and let them fertilize your prayers. Initially it may seem strange, but as you grow in grace it will become second nature and delight your heart. Keep on going. Do not let anyone discourage you, but find all your resources in the Living God who saved you. As I have said before, men will let you down, but God never fails.

Yours affectionately in Christ Jesus

WEEK SEVEN

Letter No 7:

The Greatness of God

As I have been asked to preach the gospel this Sunday I have had to think about a Bible passage to use. It struck me how essential it is to have a clear grasp of what God is like. After all, Paul in Romans 1.1 calls the message Christians proclaim "the gospel of God" (as it comes from Him and is pre-eminently about Him). A biblically ignorant society has little conception of the transcendent majesty of God. Ask anyone to name His attributes and he'd be stuck. Instead, people today create undemanding gods in their own image. Thus, in our consumer driven world, God has become whatever people want Him to be – a cosy non-judgmental God who affirms all my preferences, a God who provides cosmic therapy for my anxieties, a God who conveniently embodies all my wishes, a God who needs my support to keep going. These are all idols, manufactured by sinful men. The Bible, on the other hand, is the living eternal God's self-revelation. And God is there seen to be terrible, awesome, fearful (Psa 66.3). As someone says about Aslan in C S Lewis's story (and I quote from memory), "Safe? Who said anything about him being safe? Of course he's not safe – but he's good". No wonder the New Testament urges solemn reverence and godly fear, reminding us that "our God is a consuming fire" (Heb 12.28-29). True Christians will never be casual or thoughtless when speaking about the things of God.

All this is by way of lengthy preamble to explain why I think it might not be amiss to make this the subject of today's letter. Psalm 139 is a tremendous exposition of God's majestic greatness. Let's divide it into sections as, like any good poem, it is carefully organised. David confronts us with five truths about God:

- His infallible knowledge (vv.1-6)

- His inescapable presence (vv.7-12)
- His irresistible power (vv.13-16)
- His incomprehensible thoughts (vv.17-18)
- His inflexible righteousness (vv.19-24)

We learn first (vv.1-6) that God is **omniscient** (He knows everything). *We* acquire knowledge by study – but God knows all things intuitively and infallibly (Acts 15.18). We get things wrong (regularly, in my case!), but God is always accurate in His understanding. He knows my thoughts afar off, before they even enter my head; He knows all my ways (both my actions and my essential character); He knows each "word in my tongue", whether spoken aloud or not. It is worth noting how individual this is – God knows *me* through and through. No data protection act can hide from Him, for all is "naked and open unto the eyes of Him with whom we have to do" (Heb 4.13). Not surprisingly the psalmist is overwhelmed: "such knowledge is too wonderful for me" (v.6). And God manifest in the flesh, the Lord Jesus Christ, demonstrated this divine attribute on the earth: He knew the whole history of the Samaritan woman (John 4.29), the thoughts of men's hearts (Mark 2.6) – everything (John 16.30). We can deceive our friends, our families, ourselves – but not God. Yet what an encouragement this is to the believer! The God who loved me and saved me knew the very worst about me. Never think that the Lord was mistaken about you, or failed to take into account how you might trip up and fall short of His revealed will for you – He knew it all. And still He loved you. Read in Luke 22.31-34, 54-62 and John 21.15-17 about Peter's denial of the Lord Jesus and his subsequent restoring interview.

Our God is also **omnipresent** (vv.7-12), that is to say, He is everywhere present in His universe. There can be no escaping Him. Jonah found that by bitter experience (Jonah 1.1-2). Whether we travel as far up into space as possible or down into the heart of the earth (v.8), whether we go east to the sunrise or west to the Mediterranean (v.9), for the psalmist writes as one living in Israel, we cannot lose Him. In darkness He can still see us, for daylight and night time make no difference to Him. You see, God is not to be identified with creation (as in pantheism, as if everything were God) but is infinitely greater and grander than His universe. Again, this is a comfort to the child of God, because although the Lord Jesus Christ is at God's right hand in Heaven He is also simultaneously with each of His people (Matt 28.20; Heb 13.5). How good to know that wherever we are, "even there shall thy hand lead me, and thy right hand shall hold me" (Psa 139.10) You may be far from friends, but you will never be far from the Lord.

God is **omnipotent**, able to do anything according to His will (vv.13-16). David's specific example is creation: the God who made us is above and beyond us in His mighty power. All men's boasted achievements are only possible because God endowed them with such abilities. The exquisitely detailed language of verses 13-16 reminds us that just as God created man at the beginning, so He supervises the conception and formation of each individual child within the womb, providing for it and protecting it until the moment of delivery. A great 19th century preacher put it like this: "God saw us when we could not be seen, and He wrote about us when there was nothing of us to write about". David's reaction is worship: "I will praise thee" (v.14). We are made in God's image, distinct from every other creature, that we might enjoy Him and give Him glory. Such a God cannot fail – He is just too powerful! And He has pledged Himself to "keep you keep you from falling, and to present *you* faultless before the presence of his glory with exceeding joy" (Jude 24).

Because God's thoughts are infinite and immeasurable He is ultimately **incomprehensible** (vv.17-18). We can never fathom His greatness because our minds are not big enough. But how wonderful are God's thoughts of mercy to sinners to like us: "Let the wicked forsake his way, and the unrighteous man his thoughts: and let him return unto the LORD, and he will have mercy upon him; and to our God, for he will abundantly pardon. For my thoughts *are* not your thoughts, neither *are* your ways my ways, saith the LORD. For *as* the heavens are higher than the earth, so are my ways higher than your ways, and my thoughts than your thoughts" (Isa 55.7-9).

Finally, God is **righteous** (vv.19-24). If God will deal with the wicked it is because He is the righteous Judge of all the earth. Of ourselves we cannot satisfy His perfect standards as we fall short of His glory (Rom 3.23). But Christ Jesus became the sacrifice for sinners like you and me (Heb 10.12) that we might be brought into "the way everlasting" (v.24; John 14.6) and know God personally (John 17.3). The final verses of the psalm make a good prayer: "search me…know me…lead me". May you continue daily to learn how magnificent and glorious is the God who has saved you.

Yours affectionately in Christ Jesus

WEEK EIGHT

Letter No 8:

The Holy Spirit

Yet another of those little letters – just to try again to open up some of the riches of God's grace now that you have been saved by the precious blood of Christ. Perhaps one of the biggest problems to come up shortly after conversion is that we recognize our personal inability. Yes, my sins have been forgiven and I am right with God (and how wonderful that is!), but how ever can I live as the Lord expects me to? According to 2 Corinthians 5.17 I am a new creation in Christ Jesus, yet I still have a sinful nature and find myself falling into temptation. How can I overcome this internal conflict? How can I be what I should be for God?

The answer to this dilemma is to learn about the person and work of the Holy Spirit. You will have noted, I am sure, that the God of the Bible exists eternally in three persons. When the Lord Jesus was baptized, the Father spoke and the Spirit descended upon Him visibly like a dove (Matt 3.16-17). Believers are baptized into "the name [singular] of the Father, and of the Son, and of the Holy Spirit" (Matt 28.19). Since you are reading Ephesians chapter 2, you will have seen that our prayers are directed *to* the Father, *through* the Son, *in* the energy of the Holy Spirit (Eph 2.18). The God who has saved us is the triune God. Obviously all this is beyond the grasp of creatures because the Living God is infinitely above us. Nevertheless He graciously reveals all we need to know about Himself in His word. It may help you to think of it like this. The Father loved us and gave the Son to save us (John 3.16); the Son came into this world, adding to His deity sinless humanity that He might die for sinners like you and me (John 1.14; Gal 2.20; Heb 2.14); and the Holy Spirit is the One who takes these amazing truths and gets them into our feeble minds (John 16.13-15).

We learn from the Bible, first, that the Holy Spirit is **a real person**. Although invisible, He is as real a person as the Lord Jesus Himself. Read John 14.16-17. There the Saviour is preparing the disciples for His own departure back to heaven after the completion of His atoning work on the cross. How would they manage without His companionship? After all, He had been their teacher, their guide, their constant companion and protector. And now He was telling them He was going away – you can imagine their grief. Well, He would send "another comforter" to encourage and strengthen them during His absence. He speaks of this comforter as "He" (not "it"), for the Holy Spirit is neither a force like the wind nor an impersonal energy like electricity, but a living person with all the characteristics of personality: He thinks, wills, feels. The word "another" means another of exactly the same kind: just as the Lord Jesus had been His disciples' helper while on the earth now the Holy Spirit would take on that role, invisibly dwelling inside believers.

Second, the Holy Spirit is **a divine person**. That is to say, He possesses all the attributes that make God God. For example, He is eternal (Heb 9.14); He is infinitely holy (as His name indicates); He is sovereign in His actions (1 Cor 12.11); He is everywhere present (Psa 139.7); He was at work in creation (Gen 1.2; Job 26.13). When Ananias and Sapphira lied about the gift they were donating to the apostles, Peter told them they had lied to the Holy Spirit, but then immediately went on to say they had not lied to men but to God (Acts 5.3-4). In other words, he identified the Holy Spirit with God. Just pause and take on board the astonishing truth that this wonderful divine person in all His holiness and majesty condescends to make His home in our frail bodies. Says Paul, "know ye not that your body is the temple of the Holy Ghost *which is* in you, which ye have of God, and ye are not your own? For ye are bought with a price: therefore glorify God in your body, and in your spirit, which are God's" (1 Cor 6.19-20).

Third, the Holy Spirit is **a thoroughly active person**. In fact we can distinguish between what He does for us <u>before</u> conversion, <u>at</u> conversion and <u>after</u> conversion. Let us take the first. Before ever we were saved the Holy Spirit was at work in our hearts, convicting us of sin (John 16.8-11). That is how a sinner suddenly becomes aware that there is something desperately wrong with him. Using His sword (God's word) the Holy Spirit pricked the consciences of the Jews who listened to Peter at Pentecost (Acts 2.36-37). More, it was the Holy Spirit who organised the very circumstances of our lives so that we heard about and trusted Christ. Listen to Peter writing to converted Jews: "[you are] elect [or chosen] according to the foreknowledge of God the Father, through sanctification of the Spirit, unto obedience and sprinkling of the blood of Jesus Christ" (1 Pet 1.2). In other words, God chose them in eternity past, and the Holy Spirit set them apart for that precise moment when they obeyed the message of the gospel and came into the good of the value of the atoning death of Christ. Nothing in your pre-conversion life happened by chance – all was superintended by the Living God to draw you to Himself.

But not only did the Holy Spirit move in our hearts to lead us to Christ; the very minute we trusted Him the Holy Spirit engaged in at least four activities. When a sinner is saved he is (i) **born of the Spirit** (John 1.11; 3.5) in that it is through God's Spirit that I am regenerated (given new spiritual life). God has implanted in my heart a new set of values and desires which accord with Him. Yes, the old sinful, selfish value system (called the flesh) is still there, but I now have the potential capacity to want to do God's will, a nature which longs for His word and rejoices to have fellowship with Him and His people. Further, at the moment of conversion the believing sinner is (ii) **baptized in the Spirit** (1 Cor 12.13), in the sense that he comes personally into the good of what happed historically on the Day of Pentecost. This is not the same as water baptism, which is our act of voluntary obedience to the Saviour's command (Matt 28.18-20), but is rather a spiritual operation joining us to an entity called "the body of Christ" (the vast company of all those who belong to Christ). This baptism can neither be felt nor seen but it brings us into vital union with Christ and all His people so that you are as much a part of Him as your finger is part of your body. Again, at conversion you become (iii) **indwelt by the Spirit** (Rom 8.9), so that God's Spirit takes up His residence in your body, making it His temple. Finally, you are (iv) **sealed by the Spirit** (Eph 1.13-14). In ancient times a seal was a badge of ownership and a guarantee of security, so you are marked as God's personal property, secured "until the redemption of the purchased possession" (when the Lord comes to give us our resurrection bodies).

Thereafter the Spirit will seek produce in you those spiritual features God longs to see in you as His child. Some of them are described in Ephesians 5.18-21 (joy, thankfulness, submission) and Galatians 5.22-23 (a pen portrait of the character of the Lord Jesus Christ Himself). So do not be discouraged: you are not alone. God has given you all you need to live for His glory.

Yours affectionately in Christ Jesus

Letter No 9:

The Person of Christ

It was good to have you over the other 'day. Thanks for the visit, the strawberries and the Bruckner symphony (which I have been enjoying, although I have to confess that I feel much more at home with the precision of the Baroque than the lushness of the late-Romantic era). I much appreciated looking at Ephesians and Mark with you – you certainly drew attention to some key episodes from the Gospel. Perhaps we could continue with that next time you come over.

I thought I'd write this time about the person and work of Christ, as He is central to everything. Paul makes the point in two verses: "Grace *be* with all them that love our Lord Jesus Christ in sincerity" (Eph 6.24), and "if any man love not the Lord Jesus Christ, let him be Anathema [accursed]. Maranatha [O Lord, come!]" (1 Cor 16.22). Our relationship to Christ is crucial. And this is developed through reading the scriptures, for they are about Him: Luke 24.13-27,44; John 5.46-47. It is as we feed on the word that we encounter the Lord.

The first fact to grasp about the Lord Jesus Christ is that **He is God**. This can be demonstrated in several ways: (i) He claimed to be God (John 8.56-59, compare Exodus 3.13-14 to see that He was taking on Himself the great Old Testament name of God); (ii) the biblical writers affirm that He is God (John 1.1-3; Titus 2.13; Romans 9.5); (iii) He accepted worship as God (Heb 1.6; John 20.28-29; contrast Revelation 22.8-9); (iv) He does uniquely divine works (compare Genesis 1.1 and Hebrews 1.1-2; John 5.21-23; compare Job 9.8 and John 6.19). All this means that He is not a little less than God, or some exalted angelic being, but the Living God Himself.

The next thing to learn is that **He voluntarily became man**. Micah 5.2

speaks about His coming forth in birth from Bethlehem but also reminds us that He is simultaneously the eternal One who had no beginning. Having proved in chapter 1 that He is God (Heb 1.8), the writer of the Hebrews epistle goes on in chapter 2 to assert His genuine humanity: "Forasmuch then as the children are partakers of flesh and blood, he also himself likewise took part of the same" (Heb 2.14-15). Paul expresses it memorably like this: "God was manifest in the flesh" (1 Timothy 3.16). This is a miracle beyond comprehension – that the Living God of the universe should come into the world He had made and make Himself known to His creatures (John 1.10-12)! The language of Colossians 2.9 is astonishing: "in Him [that is, in Christ] dwelleth all the fullness of the Godhead bodily". As you read the Bible jot down the evidences of the Saviour's deity and humanity. You will assemble a huge collection of passages. All this fertilizes our worship – we praise the Saviour for His glory as God and His condescension in becoming man.

But what did the Son of God do when He entered our world? **He revealed what God is like** ("No man hath seen God at any time; the only begotten Son, which is in the bosom of the Father, he hath declared *him*", John 1.18) and demonstrated at the same time what man ought to be. You see He is both God and perfect man. So His earthly life is full of wonderful instruction and encouragement for us. Often we can see deity and manhood side by side: He slept in a boat because He was weary and yet He stilled the storm (Mark 4.38-41); He rested by the well at Sychar but also told the Samaritan woman her whole life's history (John 4.6,17-18,29); He wept at the grave of Lazarus but also raised him from the dead (John 11.35,43-44). No one could find any sin in Him for He was the spotless Lamb of God (see 1 Peter 1.19; 2.21-24; 2 Corinthians 5.21). But perfection is much more than the mere absence of evil. The Lord Jesus not only did nothing wrong, He positively did everything that was right, for He "went about doing good" (Acts 10.38). As you read Mark's Gospel you could note the gracious features of the Lord Jesus: He was just, compassionate, truthful, humble, prompt, unceasing in His labours. His miracles, words, teaching and life-style all testify to the loveliness of His person. No wonder Paul makes love for the Lord Jesus the mark of the believer (Eph 6.24).

Finally, what was the primary reason for His coming into the world? It was not just to show us what God is like, and what we ought to be. Exposing our personal sinfulness condemns us for our failure but provides no remedy. But **Christ Jesus came that He might die for His people** (Matt 1.21). Great verses say this: Hebrews 2.9 ("for the suffering of death"), 1 Timothy 1.15 ("Christ Jesus came into the world to save sinners"), Mark

10.45 ("to give his life a ransom for many"). You'll find many others. Now this should have the effect of producing the utmost love and devotion in our hearts. That the Son of God loved me and gave Himself for me demands that I respond to Him with obedience, loyalty and affection. Consider the final verse of Isaac Watts's famous hymn:

> Were the whole realm of nature mine,
> That were an offering far too small;
> Love so amazing, so divine
> Demands my life, my soul, my all.

As you get to know Him better day by day your love for Him will increase. So keep on growing and continue steadfastly (Acts 2.42).

May the living God bless and sustain you. You are always in my prayers.

Affectionately as ever in Christ Jesus

WEEK TEN

Letter No 10:

The Cross

As I am now back from Derby but do not know whether I shall see you before I head south again to Harrogate I thought I'd write another letter about a vital Christian doctrine. As you know, at the heart of the Christian faith, indeed at the centre of the gospel message, is the death of the Lord Jesus Christ. Paul says that "the preaching of the cross is to them that perish foolishness; but unto us which are saved it is the power of God" (1 Cor 1.18). But why is it so crucial? I suggest that it demonstrates a number of wonderful truths, which I hope you will pause to think about.

First, it testifies to **the accuracy of the Bible**. Speaking of His imminent death, the Lord Jesus said "for this cause came I into the world" (John 12.27). In the Old Testament the cross is anticipated in several ways. It is predicted directly in a whole series of prophecies which were amazingly fulfilled at Calvary. Somebody has estimated that about 30 came true in the last 24 hours of the Lord's earthly life. His betrayal (compare Psa 41.9 and John 13.18), suffering (compare Psa 22.16 and Matt 27.35; John 20.25), and burial (compare Isa 53.9 and Matt 27.57-60) were all preannounced in strikingly precise detail. More, God organised the history and religious life of His people Israel to picture the value of Christ's sacrificial death. For example, and there are many others, the "sacrifice" of Isaac (Gen 22.2; Heb 11.17), the Passover lamb (Exod 12.3-13; 1 Cor 5.7), the smitten rock (Exod 17.6; 1 Cor 10.4) and the brazen serpent in the wilderness (Num 21.8; John 3.14-15) all picture aspects of the work of Christ. By means of the Old Testament worship system God taught the terrible consequences of sin and the need for a blood atonement, because "without the shedding of blood is no remission" (Heb 9.22). It is therefore no surprise when we read that the Saviour was "delivered by the determinate counsel and foreknowledge of God" (Acts 2.23). The cross was no accident, no tragedy, no last-minute response to man's sin, but a vital aspect of God's eternal purpose (Luke 24.26, 44).

Second, it proves **the dreadfulness of my sin**. There is no more conclusive demonstration of man's wickedness than Calvary: God sent His Son into the world to display His heart of love, yet men would not have Him (John 15.23-25; Acts 10.38-39). "The more closely we look at the Lord Jesus on earth, at His path here, and at what He met with in that path, the more we see the terrible alienation of men's hearts from God". It is not Sodom or Belsen which proves our depravity, but Calvary, in which all men representatively had a part: "against thy holy child Jesus, whom thou hast anointed, both Herod, and Pontius Pilate, with the Gentiles, and the people of Israel, were gathered together" (Acts 4.27).

Third, it illustrates the **obedience of the Son to the Father**. The gospel records show that the Lord Jesus came to do His Father's will. The Old Testament gives us a foretaste of this in Psalm 40.8 ("I delight to do thy will, O God"), a claim which the New Testament locks into the experience of Christ (Heb 10.9). Now the Lord's obedience "unto death, even the death of the cross" (Phil 2.5-8) was not the absence of strength, as though He had no ability to resist man's wickedness; rather, it was divine strength of character to accept God's eternal purpose for Him whatever the cost, without question, without objection and without resentment. You have only to read John chapter 18 (the astonishing account of His arrest) to see that He could have escaped the suffering. He made no effort to hide from the soldiers who came to apprehend Him (v.4); He had only to speak the words "I am" (but look at Exodus 3.13-14 to grasp their significance) to have the entire band of men fall prostrate before Him (v.6); and He even ensured that His disciples received a safe conduct out of the garden (vv.8-9). It is therefore abundantly clear that He allowed them to take Him and lead Him away (vv.12-13). He thus becomes our pattern of self-denying devotedness to the will of God. May we be obedient children (Rom 6.17).

Fourth, the cross spells **the defeat of Satan**. In Genesis 3.15 the very first announcement of the cross places it in the context of the Devil's judgment. While he would be able to bruise the seed of the woman's heel (a minor wound – death) that seed (Christ) would bruise Satan's head (a major blow). This is expanded in Hebrews 2.14-15. You see, the work of the cross was a triumphant victory. Although Satan's final overthrow awaits the Saviour's return (see Romans 16.20 and Revelation 20.10) he has already been robbed of his power in that we, who once were under his dominion, have been set free by the Lord Jesus (Eph 2.1-6).

Fifth – and this is what touches us most immediately – the cross provides **the salvation of believing sinners**. It is God's answer to our sinfulness, because it allows Him to be absolutely just (in that He poured out on the person of Christ my substitute all His righteous judgement against my sin) while simultaneously declaring me judicially free. The cross vindicates God's righteousness yet exhausts His wrath as far as the believer is concerned, for "the Lord hath laid on him [Christ] the iniquity of us all" (Isa 53.6). How much we should praise God for devising a way of salvation which brings such glory to His name. Keep on growing, and may the Living God who loves you sustain you daily by His grace and power.

Affectionately as always in Christ Jesus

WEEK ELEVEN

Letter No 11:

The Lord's Return

Let me write to you about another great teaching in the Bible - that the Saviour who came once to die for our sins is coming back to the world which rejected Him. One of the great things about being saved is that not only do we know where we came from (Gen 1.26-28; we are created by and for God), and why we are here (Eph 1.12; to glorify His name), we also know exactly where we are going (John 14.3; to be with Christ Jesus for ever). History has a purpose and a goal, organised by the God who works all things after the counsel of His will (Eph 1.11).

It becomes clear as you read the Bible that God has a programme. The moment sin entered the world He announced the coming of a Deliverer to deal with Satan (Gen 3.15); and thereafter gradually provided fuller information about that Deliverer in the Old Testament books of history, poetry and prophecy. He would be a genuine man ("the seed of the woman", Gen 3.15), a descendant of Abraham via Isaac (Gen 12.1-3; 21.12; Rom 9.7), from the tribe of Judah (Gen 49.10) and the royal family of David (2 Sam 7.12-16), born specifically at Bethlehem (Mic 5.2). In fact, one could sum up the whole of the Old Testament in the phrase from its final book, "Behold, He shall come" (Mal 3.1). And in due time, of course, the Lord Jesus came to earth (Gal 4.4), and was recognised as the promised Deliverer: "We have found him, of whom Moses in the law, and the prophets, did write, Jesus of Nazareth, the son of Joseph" (John 1.45). So the Redeemer has come. But wait. The New Testament insists that the Lord Jesus will come a second time (Heb 9.28; John 14.3). Indeed, even the first prediction of His arrival back in Genesis 3.15 intimates two distinct activities: His heel would be bruised by the serpent (which happened at Calvary), but He in turn would bruise the serpent's head (which Romans 16.20 places in the future, awaiting His return in glory to deal finally with sin and Satan). So the Old Testament distinguishes between the first and second comings of the Saviour, although that distinction is not clearly appreciated until we get to the New Testament.

The return of the Lord Jesus will take place in two great stages. **FIRST**, He will come *into the air* to catch up to Himself all those who belong to Him. Christians often call this event **the rapture**, going back to the etymological meaning of the word, because the Greek term used by Paul in 1 Thessalonians 4.13-18 ("we which are alive *and* remain shall be caught up [*harpazo*]") signifies to snatch or catch away. You could search the New Testament with e-sword to see how this interesting word is used elsewhere – for example Acts 8.39 and 23.10. This event will involve (i) a resurrection of all dead believers of this age, and (ii) an instantaneous removal from earth of all living believers. Both groups will meet the Lord Jesus Christ in the air to be for ever with Him. Lest anyone attempt to reduce this language to metaphor, Paul grounds it upon the historicity of the Saviour's first coming: "if we believe that Jesus died and rose again" (1 Thess 4.14). Yes, He did truly die, and rise again from the dead – the reality of those great miracles in past time and space are the pledge that He will return from heaven to take His people home. If the Son of the Living God could take on Himself sinless humanity, enter into death for me, and rise again – I really can have no difficulty believing that He can come back! Further, we shall meet the Lord not as we are now but in glorified bodies: that is the great point of Paul's teaching in 1 Corinthians, which harmonizes perfectly with 1 Thessalonians:

> "Behold, I shew you a mystery [something never disclosed in the Old Testament]; we shall not all sleep [die], but we shall all be changed [transformed], in a moment, in the twinkling of an eye, at the last trump: for the trumpet shall sound, and the dead shall be raised incorruptible [dead Christians resurrected], and we shall be changed [living Christians transformed]. For this corruptible must put on incorruption, and this mortal *must* put on immortality" (1 Cor 15.51-53).

God will not be satisfied until He has given you a body like the glorious body of His Son! "[He] shall change our vile body, that it may be fashioned like unto his glorious body, according to the working whereby he is able even to subdue all things unto himself" (Phil 3.20-21). Now this is an eminently practical truth – it gives me a sure hope for the future (1 Thess 1.9-10), it is a motivation for godly living (1 John 3.2-3) and Christian service (Luke 19.13), and it reminds me that as a citizen of heaven I do not belong down here (Phil 3.20).

SECOND, the Lord will come back *to the very earth* where He was crucified. Whereas the rapture involves our removal from the world, the second stage of the Saviour's return (often called the **revelation**) means that He will touch down on the planet. It is the ascension reversed: "this same Jesus. . .shall so come in like manner as ye have seen him go into heaven" (Acts 1.11). As He left from the Mount of Olives so will He return (see Acts 1.12; Zech 14.1-4). This glorious public coming of Christ to judge His enemies, rescue Israel and establish His kingdom over the earth, is taught in the Old Testament (Zechariah 14 is clear, but see too Isa 9.6-7; Luke 1.31-33; Jer 23.5-8; 33.14-17; Hosea 3.4-5) as well as the New (Matt 24.29-31; Rev 1.7; 19.11-21; 20.1-6). You might like especially to consider the Lord's use of Isaiah 61.1-2 in His synagogue reading in Luke 4.16-21 (where He stops in mid-verse and closes the book – the part of the prophecy He read was fulfilled that day, but there is more to come in the future). The MacArthur Study Bible notes will help. The Lord's coming to take us home is imminent (that is to say, as far as we are concerned it could happen at any moment), but His public coming to earth will only be after the terrible period of the Great Tribulation (Matt 24.29; see the horrific details in Revelation chapters 6-19). Be all the more thankful that you belong by grace to the God in charge of history, and live in the light of the Saviour's soon return for us.

Affectionately as always in Christ Jesus

WEEK TWELVE

Letter No 12:

Trials

It was so good to see you this afternoon and have a little time of fellowship with you around God's word. Thanks for taking me into 1 Peter chapter 1 which, as you say, is really packed with interesting and challenging truth. Since one of its great themes is suffering, I thought I'd write to you on that topic. Too many folk seem to think that to be saved is to be freed from troubles. On the contrary, salvation involves suffering in this world precisely because we belong to the Lord Jesus.

The Bible leaves us under no illusion about **the certainty of trials.** Peter tells his readers to "think it not strange" (1 Pet 4.12) when they fall into different kinds of difficulty. These difficulties include persecution from a hostile world, sinful temptation from inside, and adverse circumstances which may shake our faith. Three distinct words are used in the New Testament. One is "tribulation [*thlipsis*]", which means pressure or stress (Acts 14.22). The Saviour frankly warned His disciples that "in the world *ye shall have* tribulation" (John 16.33). We should of course distinguish between the common lot of God's people in all ages and that future unique period of trouble on earth called the Great Tribulation (Matt 24.21; Rev 7.14), a period from which Christians are exempted (1 Thess 5.9). Another word is "temptation [*peirasmos*]", which means proving, testing, trying. This, says Paul, is "common to man" (1 Cor 10.13). The third is "training [*paideia*]", which refers to the disciplining of children. God, the perfect Father, disciplines "every son whom He receiveth" (Heb 12.6-8). Clearly, trials are an inescapable aspect of the Christian pathway down here. We all have to climb Hill Difficulty – often many times.

Further, God's word is honest about **the seriousness of trials.** In the Old Testament Job is the great "example of suffering affliction" (James 5.10-

11). This man of God suffered materially, losing in one fell swoop "all that he hath" (Job 1.11), that is, his possessions (1.15-17), his children (1.18-19), and his wife's support (2.9). But he also suffered physically in "his bone and his flesh" (2.5), being afflicted with a disease that was unsightly (2.12), uncomfortable (2.8) and incurable. Some illnesses are dignified: not so Job's boils.

But the Bible goes much further than this and rips back the curtain to display **the source of trials**. We look around and recognise that there may sometimes be human instrumentality involved in our sufferings (Job 1.15; Luke 22.55-60). Job was robbed by the Sabeans, Peter was put to the test by two men and a servant girl. The incompetence of a doctor, the malice of a fellow-worker, the folly of a drunken driver – these may lie at the root of our distress. We can also look beneath to glimpse Satanic animosity against the people of God (Job 1.9-12; Luke 22.31; 13.16). In Job's case, Satan was behind his disasters. But we must never lose sight of the fact that in the final analysis all our circumstances are governed by God Himself. As the psalmist says, "Thou hast afflicted me" (Psa 88.7; 119.75; Amos 3.6). In other words we are to look above and acknowledge divine sovereignty. Since the ultimate authority in the universe is God alone we can trace all to His hand, knowing that "whoever brings an affliction it is God that sends it" (Psa 66.8-12; Eph 1.11). It was God who gave Satan permission to attack Job. And Job bore unembittered testimony to this when he said "The Lord gave and the Lord [not the Sabeans, or Satan] hath taken away" (Job 1.21; 1 Sam 2.6-7). But finally we must look within to cultivate personal accountability, for although we are not responsible for all the circumstances of our lives we are answerable for the way we respond to them. They can make us bitter (Job 2.9; 2 Chron 28.22-25; Rev 16.9), releasing resentment, impatience and rebellion; or they can make us better (Rom 5.3; 2 Sam 22.7; Psa 118.5), developing in us dependence, acceptance, obedience, and endurance.

That leads on inevitably to the next point: **the strategy of trials**. God has a gracious aim in all that befalls His people. James encourages us to see "the end [purpose] of the Lord" in his dealings with Job (Jas 5.11; Job 42.12; Rom 8.28-30). There are many aspects to this purpose but here are some. God aims to reveal our ability by grace to endure more than we ever thought we could (Job 1.8-12; 2.3; 13.15; Hab 3.17); to refine our faith by testing just as a precious metal is purified by fire (Job 23.10; 1 Pet 1.7); to regulate and bring us back into line when we drift away from Him (Heb 12.4-13; Psa 119.67,71); and to reward our faithfulness in the future (Jas 1.12; Heb 10.32-37). In other words, our afflictions down here encourage us to look ahead to the Lord's return. This reminds us that God is not now primarily in the business of dealing with the body (Rom 8.22-23) but moulding the character. He plans to make us like His Son, and suffering is His great educational tool. Those who constantly crave physical healing are out of line with God's revealed purpose.

Finally, we can rejoice that God has graciously provided support agencies to help us through our afflictions. Divine **support for trials** is found as we read the scriptures (1 Cor 10.1-11; Rom 15.4; James 5.10) to see how earlier saints were sustained through their sufferings. Further, we can rely constantly on a "God [who] is faithful" (1 Cor 10.13) and will not suffer us to be tested beyond our endurance. We should gather with the saints, enjoying the encouragement of local assembly fellowship (Acts 4.23; Heb 10.23-5), learning to react spiritually to our problems (1 Cor 10.13b). God will grant us either the grace of avoidance to get out (as Joseph did when faced with solicitation to evil in Genesis 39.12) or the grace of acceptance to go through (as Job did). In God's goodness, the most painful circumstances can actually strengthen us spiritually. Take this on board, for you will need it in days to come. May the Lord continue daily to bless and sustain you by His grace.

Affectionately as always in Christ Jesus

WEEK THIRTEEN

Letter No 13:

Miracles

I was delighted to see the other day that you are continuing to enjoy the scriptures – there is nothing more valuable for the believer. Your alternation between New Testament letters and Gospels will provide quite a balanced diet. As you say, each time you reread a part of the Bible you will discover that it contains more riches than you detected first time round. John especially always strikes me as a Tardis-like book – there's much more inside than initially meets the eye!

Since John 5 started off with an important miracle of healing and caused us to spend a while discussing the Lord's miracles generally I thought I'd attempt a little summary of what we should know about them. Of course, there are and have been plenty of religious frauds, but the very first thing to say about the Lord's earthly miracles is that they were **genuine**. That is Peter's claim at Pentecost (Acts 2.22), appealing to his hearers' topical knowledge. They were performed in public before many often hostile witnesses (Luke 5.17,21,26). They were testable by outsiders; indeed, far from frowning on external investigation, the Lord Jesus often made sure that His miracles were rigorously scrutinised (John 2.6-10; Matt 8.4). They were performed in the context of daily life – not in some purpose-built stadium amidst all the emotional razzmatazz of a healing meeting, but by the sea shore, in a busy street, in a home. But, second, these miracles were **spectacular**. "The very essence of a miracle is God rising above all circumstances" (William Kelly). Certainly the Lord's deeds provoked amazement among the beholders, for He had power over the elements, disease, death, demons. And His healings were *instantaneous*, never requiring convalescence, as Mark signals with his distinctive word "immediately" (Mark 1.31,42; 2.12; 5.29,42), *indisputable* (in that those most eager to demean the Lord Jesus never attempted to deny that He worked wonders; Mark 2.12;3.22; John 11.47) and *infallible* (for He had no failures; Matt 9.35; 12.15). In other words, these were miracles worthy of God. Someone has said that a New Testament without the miracles would be easier to believe – trouble is, it would not be worth believing.

Third, they were **abundant**. We must not assume that the Lord worked them on rare occasions; rather, they were the characteristic feature of His ministry for, as John says, "many other signs truly did Jesus" (20.30). It seems that wherever He went sickness and death were banished from Israel. Just consider Matthew's repeated summary statements (4.23-24; 8.16; 9.35; 12.15; 14.14,35-36; 15.29-31). And John tells us that many more signs were left unrecorded in scripture (20.30-31; 21.25). Fourth, the Lord's miracles were manifestly **divine** (John 3.2; Acts 2.22; 10.38). You see, the Bible frankly acknowledges the possibility of satanic marvels, for the mere fact of the supernatural does not of itself guarantee that God is the immediate source. Pharaoh's magicians could replicate some of Moses' miracles in Exodus 7 and 8, Simon the Sorcerer had considerable power (Acts 8.9-11), and the future "Man of Sin" will perform "lying wonders" (2 Thess 2.8-12). Those who crave the spectacular today should bear in mind the Lord's solemn warning in Matthew 7.22-23: miracles are no proof of conversion. That is why back in Deuteronomy 13.1-5 the great test is doctrinal conformity to what God has already revealed. Even the Lord's wondrous works cannot be divorced from His sinless life and unique teaching. All He did was "in my Father's name" (John 5.43), bringing glory to God. Fifth, His miracles were all **signs** (Heb 2.3-4; John 12.37-40), evidences accrediting Him as God's long promised Messiah. His works proved He came from God (John 5.36).

Sixth, they were **anticipatory**: "powers of the age to come" (Heb 6.5). In this sense, as someone has said, "miracles are not a breach of the laws of nature but ...the bringing back of order into a disordered world". The three and a half years of the Saviour's earthly ministry in Israel were like a miniature millennium, for His signs demonstrated His ability to bring about those glorious conditions which the Old Testament predicted would accompany the great messianic age of the kingdom (see, for example, Isaiah 35.5-7 and Matthew 11.3-5). That kingdom awaits the Lord's return, but was temporarily glimpsed in His first coming. Seventh, they were **benevolent**: He "went about doing good" (Acts 10.38).The theologian BB Warfield writes, "When our Lord came down to earth He drew heaven with Him". Because His first coming was primarily in grace not judgment (John 3.17), all His dealings with men were tender, kindly and merciful. Think of Him deigning to touch the outcast leper whose terrible condition debarred him from human contact (Matt 8.3). Eighth, His miracles were **revelatory**, displaying in a visible way the character of the invisible God (John 1.18; 14.9-11). He who could touch a leper Himself remained perfectly undefiled because He was the Holy One of God.

Ninth, His miracles were **illustrative** of what He can do for poor sinners. As you said the other day, the story recorded in Mark 2.1-12 is the great key to understanding all the miracles. The priority was clearly to deal with sins; that is why He came (1 Tim 1.15). But because the forgiveness of sins cannot be registered by mortal eyes He graciously worked a physical miracle: He who can cure the paralytic can also pardon my sins! In this sense all the Lord's miracles are gospel messages – they teach the ruin of man (disabled by sin) and the gracious remedy of God (delivered into new life by Christ). Finally (and this may seem odd) His earthly miracles were **restricted**: limited to a short period of public ministry (John 2.11), to the tiny land of Israel (Acts 10.39), to a human life-span (for Lazarus died again!) You see, miracles were never the main thing but only pointers to His person and atoning work on the cross. Our salvation is a grander work by far for it lasts for ever (John 10.27-28)! May the Lord encourage you to keep going day by day.

Affectionately as always in Christ Jesus

Letter No 14:

Baptism

Since you mentioned baptism last time we met I thought I'd just sum up the Bible's teaching on this important subject. I know you have John Ritchie's useful booklet and other material I have given you in the past, but it can do no harm to précis the truth. So here's the acrostic outline I think I used when a mutual friend was baptized at Eastpark Gospel Hall some years ago.

The **Basis** for baptism is simply the authority of the scriptures. Why should you get baptized? Not because of some church tradition, or because I recommend it, but because the Bible says so (Matt 28.18-20). Your faith must be grounded on the rock-solid reliability of God's infallible word, not on the teaching of men or even the prompting of friends. Subject everything you hear or read to the acid test of scripture: the Bereans' safety lay in the fact that they "searched the scriptures daily, [to see] whether those things were so", measuring even an apostle's preaching against the rule of the word (Acts 17.11). Men will let you down – the Bible, never. Paul rejoiced that when the Thessalonians "received the word of God which ye heard of us, ye received *it* not *as* the word of men, but as it is in truth, the word of God, which effectually worketh also in you that believe" (1 Thess 2.13). Again, at Corinth "my speech and my preaching *was* not with enticing words of man's wisdom, but in demonstration of the Spirit and of power: that your faith should not stand in the wisdom of men, but in the power of God" (1 Cor 2.4-5).

The physical **Action** involved is immersion in water. That is evident from the sense of the Greek word *baptizo* (transliterated rather than translated into English as "baptize"), which, as you will see if you check your e-Sword Thayer, means to dip or plunge. The places where it happened also support this (John 3.23). Sprinkling or pouring could have been easily effected by means of the Ethiopian's water bottle; instead he and Philip found a pool and "went down both into the water" (Acts 8.36-9).

The **People** baptized in New Testament times were always professing believers in the Lord Jesus Christ. The Bible teaches neither infant nor adult but believers' baptism (Acts 2.41; 8.12; 18.8). The sequence "believe and be baptized" (Mark 16.16) is inviolable.

But is the action arbitrary? Far from it: built into baptism is clear **Teaching** about God's salvation. Like a visual aid it testifies to death (we go into the water), burial (we go under the water; see Jonah 2.3b) and resurrection (we come out of the water), proclaiming both what Christ did for sinners like us (1 Cor 15.3-4), and the fact that by grace we have come into the good of it. Remember that baptism does not actually do anything to you apart from make you wet – it simply illustrates what happened when you were saved. By baptism I am identified with what Christ did for me. As a pictorial burial it witnesses to the ending of my old pre-conversion life and the beginning of "newness of life" in Christ (Rom 6.1-6). No wonder this was the first thing folk did after they were saved! It announced to all that they were under new management.

Nor is it an optional extra. The biblical language is consistently **Imperative**. The Lord instructed His apostles to baptize new converts as an essential part of their spiritual education (Matt 28.18-20). Thus Peter did not advise Cornelius and his household; rather, once it was clear they had trusted the Saviour "he <u>commanded</u> them to be baptized in the name of the Lord" (Acts 10.48). We do not have to wait for some deep inner feeling in order to obey: the command is sufficient. "Whatsoever he saith unto you, do *it*" (John 2.8).

Further, it is a solemn **Signal** announcing my intention to follow the Saviour all the way. All those baptized at Pentecost also "continued steadfastly" with the other disciples "in the apostles' doctrine and fellowship, and in breaking of bread, and in prayers" (Acts 2.42). Although you are not baptized into a church, the biblical expectation is that, like Saul, you will join yourself to a company of God's people meeting in accordance with His directions (Acts 9.18-19). In other words, baptism is not the end – rather, it marks the beginning of a lifetime's submission to the word.

Finally, let us return to that first question. *Why* get baptized? Because the Bible says so – yes, *and also* because we love the Lord Jesus (1 John 4.19).

The presiding **Motive** for every act of Christian obedience is love (John 15.14; 14.15) – indeed, it is only by our obedience that we demonstrate the reality of our love for Him who died for us.

Well, there's your little outline, carefully condensed as usual on to an A4 page! It is my prayer that the Lord will continue to uphold you daily by His gracious power, leading you in His paths of righteousness. Do get in touch and arrange a visit when you can.

Affectionately as always in Christ Jesus

Letter No 15:

The Local Church

Since we shall not meet until next week I thought I'd summarise some of the principles underlying a New Testament local church. You will soon discover that many dear believers who are perfectly happy to trust the Bible when it comes to their soul's salvation part company with it thereafter. However, if I can believe God's word in the urgent matter of my eternal destiny does it not make sense also to follow its instructions about Christian conduct and worship as we wait the Lord's return to take us home to glory? After all, since the Lord Jesus purchased me with His shed blood He alone has the right to tell me how to behave. It is therefore not a matter of choosing a church according to personal preference or family tradition or simple convenience. As always, the key question is "What saith the scripture?" (Rom 4.3; Gal 4.30)

Last time I attempted an acrostic on baptism, so here in similar vein is a précis of what the Bible says about a local church. Please remember to check all I say for yourself because I want you to get your own convictions from the word. Never believe unthinkingly what any man says – be like the Bereans and search the scriptures daily (Acts 17.11). Of course, every believer in the Lord Jesus is a member of what the Bible calls "the body of Christ" (Eph 1.22-23; 3.6; 1 Cor 12.13) from the very instant of conversion. That is, whether they know it or not, all saved people have been eternally joined to the Saviour and thus belong to that vast invisible company of the redeemed of this age. That is part and parcel of salvation. But entering a local church is another matter which requires a personal exercise.

First, a local church is a **Company** of people rather than a building or a religious institution (Acts 5.11; 11.22,26). As they say, a church is not a steeple but a people. The word *ekklesia* means "assembly", a company of folk called out for a particular purpose. Read through the book of the Acts to notice how remarkably uninterested Luke is in the actual buildings in which believers met. Each local church is an autonomous company, responsible not to an earthly headquarters but to the risen Lord Jesus Christ. That is why we never read in the New Testament about "the church of Judea" or "the church of Galatia" (suggesting organisations like the Church of Scotland) but "the churches [plural] of Judea/Galatia" (Gal 1.2,22). Everywhere the apostles went they preached the gospel and planted independent companies of believers who, though enjoying fellowship together, were accountable directly to their Saviour (Acts 14.21-23).

Second, it is a **Holy** company, because it is restricted to genuine Christian membership. On the day of Pentecost those who responded positively to Peter's preached message were baptized, "added" to the existing company of believers and then "continued steadfastly" with them in their spiritual exercises (Acts 2.41-42). Paul refers to "churches of God/Christ" (1 Thess 2.14; Rom 16.16), indicating their ownership and origin, and "churches of the saints [that is, holy or set apart ones]" (1 Cor 14.33), testifying to their saved character. A church is no religious club which anyone can join but a divinely authorised gathering of saved people who constitute a "holy temple" for God's glory (1 Cor 3.16-17). Paul's language here is very solemn. In verses 6 to 17 he recounts the founding of the church at Corinth, reminding his readers that they were either building up or damaging a work of God. This has consequences: what I do to the local assembly in which He has placed me God will do to me. To come into the fellowship of God's people in a local assembly is therefore a serious responsibility involving real commitment of soul (Acts 9.26-28).

Third, it is a **United** company, held together not by a dominating human personality or by a denominational creed but by (i) unconditional submission to the scriptures (Acts 2.42; 20.32) and (ii) heartfelt allegiance to the person of Christ (Phil 2.1-5; Eph 6.24). After all, an assembly gathers to His name (Matt 18.20): it meets in accordance with His teaching and in acknowledgement of His presence in the midst. Where His people gather to Him, there the Saviour is! Christians do not gather primarily to hear a preacher but to meet the Lord. That is why we should, if at all possible, never miss the gatherings of the saints (Heb 10.24-25).

Fourth, it is a **Regulated** company. Far from being a free-for-all where anything goes, it is governed by the unchanging teachings of God's word and the shepherd care of local elders. A local church does not conform to the passing fashions of the world. For example, because the Bible makes a distinction between the function of males and females (one traceable back to the very way in which God created us), Christian women cover their heads while Christian men do not. Paul explains this spiritual symbolism in 1 Corinthians 11.2-16. Again, in chapter 14.34-37 he restricts vocal participation in the gatherings to the men folk – not because they are superior to the sisters but because God says so. There were no salaried clergymen in New Testament times; instead, God raised up in each assembly older spiritual men with a love for the word and a concern for the saints. When Paul addressed the elders of the Ephesian church (Acts 20.17) he told them to "take heed therefore unto yourselves, and to all the flock, over the which the Holy Ghost hath made you overseers, to feed the church of God, which he hath purchased with his own blood" (Acts 20.28). Three important words come together here: assembly leaders are "elders" (indicating spiritual maturity), "overseers" (*episkopos* is often translated "bishop" in the AV but simply means one who watches over) and implicitly "shepherds" (because they feed and tend God's flock; see 1 Peter 5.1-5).

Fifth, it is a **Caring** company, likened to a body in which each member feels a genuine concern for the others (1 Cor 12.25-26). The metaphor of the body dominates 1 Corinthians 12, where Paul insists that every saint is equipped by the Holy Spirit to function for God in the local church. There should therefore be no envy (1 Cor 12.15-16), no monopoly (v.17), no independence (v.21), and no pride (v.22), because God has designed a wonderful variety within unity (vv.13-14) so that all His people can work together for His glory and their mutual blessing. There is no better sphere in which to witness and exhibit Christian graces, no better school in which to grow spiritually, than the local assembly. Indeed, the Bible knows no higher court of appeal in spiritual things on the earth (Matt 18.15-17).

Finally, it is a **Heavenly** company, appealing only to a spiritual appetite. There is nothing for the unregenerate man in assembly gatherings – no entertainment, no sports, no exciting music, no high-powered marketing techniques, no impressive ritual or ceremony. All is simple and spiritual, so as to cast the spotlight upon the person and work of Christ. At the Lord's Supper believers just gather to remember the Saviour in His own appointed way with a loaf and cup (1 Cor 11.17-34), spending the time considering the excellencies of His person and the infinite value of His work. And that is a foretaste of our eternal occupation with Christ (Rev 22.3-4).

Affectionately as always in Christ Jesus

Letter No 16:

The Pilgrim's Progress (i)

I was thinking the other day about Bunyan's *Pilgrim's Progress*. If you have not yet read it, you really ought to do so. As well as an exciting and doctrinally exact storyline, picturing for us in the most vivid terms the ups and downs of the Christian life, it contains a remarkable gallery of character types, accurately reflecting the different kinds of people one meets on the Christian pathway. Some of them are genuine believers (Faithful, Hopeful, Mr Fearing, Mr Little-Faith), some out and out enemies of the gospel (Mr Atheist, you will find, is travelling in entirely the wrong direction), some cunningly deceptive fakes (Mr Worldly-Wiseman, Mr By-Ends). Taking a leaf from his book I thought I'd try to introduce you to some folk you are likely to encounter in your pilgrimage, and in the process warn both you and me against becoming like them. You see, not everyone will be a help to us. Always remember that our model is not failing saints but the Saviour Himself: for "even hereunto were ye called: because Christ also suffered for us, leaving us an example, that ye should follow his steps" (1 Pet 2.21).

The first one is a genuine Bunyan character – **Mr Talkative**. He is remarkably widespread. This is the man who claims to be saved, rather likes being in Christian company, loves talking at great length about doctrinal matters, but whose life does not match up to his words. He is all talk and no walk. Jeremiah encountered people like that, people who sounded pious by asking for prayer but who were in reality determined to go their own way regardless of God's word (Jer 42.1-3, 20-22; 43.1-4). Time is usually the great test, and time certainly proved what was in their hearts. When the Lord Jesus was on the earth He took up the language of Isaiah's indictment of Old Testament Israel in order to expose the failure of contemporary religious leaders:

> "*Ye* hypocrites, well did Esaias prophesy of you, saying, This people draweth nigh unto me with their mouth, and honoureth me with *their* lips; but their heart is far from me" (Matt 15.8-9).

It is best to be wary of people who boast about their own spirituality. Those who are full of themselves seldom have room for anybody else. One of the most humbling experiences of the Christian life is to discover just how bad we really are inside – even *after* conversion. We have nothing to be smug about. As Paul says, "He that glorieth, let him glory in the Lord" (1 Cor 1.31). Real love for the Saviour is demonstrated not through impressive words or pious claims but through simple obedience to His commands, however unfashionable or costly (John 14.15; 15.14).

Another figure on the road might be **Mr Outward Appearance**. He is strong on externals, and swift to upbraid anyone who does not wear the clothing he approves, carry the edition of the Bible he endorses, or attend the gatherings he patronizes. Trouble is, as the Lord told Samuel, "*the LORD seeth* not as man seeth; for man looketh on the outward appearance, but the LORD looketh on the heart" (1 Sam 15.8). As so often, it is back to the heart, the biblical core of our being (Prov 4.23). An impeccable exterior, you see, may conceal a dirty soul. Of course, a correct outside *is* important. Therefore the believer will be baptized (an external act) because the Lord commands it. But the believer will also want to make certain, by the grace of God, that he is living daily a life that is "dead indeed unto sin but alive unto God" (Rom 6.1-11). It is all too easy to focus upon the outside and forget the inside. That was a particular failing of the Pharisees:

> "Woe unto you, scribes and Pharisees, hypocrites! for ye are like unto whited sepulchres, which indeed appear beautiful outward, but are within full of dead *men's* bones, and of all uncleanness. Even so ye also outwardly appear righteous unto men, but within ye are full of hypocrisy and iniquity" (Matt 23.27-28).

I can slip into cosy self-complacency simply because I am attending the meetings of my local assembly and dutifully taking part in public prayer and Bible teaching. Yet my heart may be cold as ice towards God. It is important to remember that though we may be able to fool others, our God knows us through and through: "The heart *is* deceitful above all *things*, and desperately wicked: who can know it? I the LORD search the heart, *I* try the reins, even to give every man according to his ways, *and* according to the fruit of his doings" (Jer 17.9-10). May we cultivate a real heart for God.

Another person along the journey might be **Mr Shallow**. He is the Lord's, but seems never to have grown beyond the basic facts of the gospel message. He can see nothing else in scripture. Having trusted the Saviour he promptly sits down to bask in the sunshine of forgiveness, never appreciating that God redeems us that we might honour Him by intelligent, obedient service. Thankful that "the Son of man came to seek ...that which is lost" (Luke 19.10) he forgets that the Father seeks worshippers (John 4.23). God wishes us to be mature sons, not perpetually baby saints for whom His inexhaustible word is a closed book (Eph 1.15-23). As a consequence, rarely will Mr Shallow raise his voice in worship because he has not learned to think of Calvary as anything more than the payment for his sins. But when the Lord Jesus died He not only received from God's hand all that was due to me (punishment) but also rendered to God all that was due to Him (devoted obedience unto death). As we mature in grace we become more and more taken up with the beauties of the Lord Jesus – not just what He has done for us but what He is in Himself as the most glorious person in the universe.

A distant cousin of Mr Shallow is **Mr Trivial**. Mr Trivial has no appetite for solid Bible teaching – he finds it too tedious and too demanding both intellectually and spiritually. He would much rather be at a social evening, or a "Christian" concert, where he can combine a smattering of the things of God with a hefty dose of the world. He will often hang around with a large company of similar folk his own age who are never likely to challenge his lifestyle. An assembly which tries to put into practice the teachings of the word will seem "narrow", "old-fashioned" and "dead" to Mr Trivial. Only entertainment and excitement will hold him. But where there is a genuine work of grace in the heart there will always be an unquenchable thirst for God's word (1 Pet 1.22 – 2.3). It is, alas, so hard to get people to come to a gathering where God is the only attraction – but that is what a New Testament assembly is. It gathers to the name of Christ alone and honours Him.

Seek your friends from among those who truly love the Lord and His word. Paul's advice cannot be bettered: "Flee also youthful lusts: but follow righteousness, faith, charity, peace, with them that call on the Lord out of a pure heart" (2 Tim 2.22). Good company will keep you going fervently in the Lord despite discouragement and difficulty. So press onwards on the journey!

Affectionately as always in Christ Jesus

WEEK SEVENTEEN

Letter No 17:

The Authority of the Bible

Time for another letter! I was looking though the subjects that I have already dealt with and one of the surprising omissions is the authority of scripture. So that is today's topic. And it is of enormous practical consequence because everything else in the Christian life follows from it. That is why it is often the first subject in a book about doctrine. After all, if the Bible is not true, we have no reliable, objective source of information about God, about ourselves, about the origin and future of this universe.

First we should note the Bible's **singularity** – there is just no book like it. Paul refers to the "holy [*hieros*, meaning 'sacred, consecrated to God'] scriptures", which are "given by inspiration of God" or, more literally, "God-breathed" (2 Tim 3.14-17). It is not that existing writings were breathed into by God but that the scriptures are themselves the very breath of His mouth. They are His voice. Years ago one of my unbelieving student friends at Oxford took a Bible out of his college library and, compelled to record the author's name in the register, wrote "God". He told me this with a smile – but he was right. Although often dismissed as a circular argument, it is surely not insignificant that the book insistently claims divine origin (2 Pet 1.21; Matt 19.4-5; 1 Cor 14.37). Indeed, in the Old Testament the phrase "thus saith the Lord" occurs something like 2,500 times. Despite all attempts to outlaw and destroy it, from the Emperor Diocletian to Richard Dawkins, it survives. They say that about 80% of books are forgotten after the first year and only half are in demand seven years later, but a book whose earliest portion was penned about 3500 years ago is still a best seller. Not surprising, since it is uniquely able to make us "wise unto salvation".

Second, observe its **unity**. In 2 Timothy 3. 14-17 Paul writes both of the "scriptures" (plural) and "scripture" (singular). Although consisting of 66 books written by some 40 authors from 13 countries in 3 languages over a period of about 1600 years it remains one coherent whole, held together from start from finish by a consistency of theme and outlook. And the presiding theme is the person of Christ Himself, the living eternal Word (Luke 24.25-27,44-45; John 1.1). The Old Testament's constant anticipation of the coming of a Deliverer finds its realisation in the gospels where the Saviour visits planet earth (Matt 1.1; John 1.45), yet that amazing visit is only fully explained in the New Testament letters, where Paul tells us *why* the Lord Jesus came and died (1 Tim 1.15). Because it so tightly coheres, it is often rightly said that every question the Bible raises, the Bible answers. Difficulties there may be, but these can be resolved as we read more of God's word, for each part illuminates the whole.

Another piece of evidence is its **accuracy**. The psalmist was prepared to take his stand on the unchanging truth of the word: "For ever, O LORD, thy word is settled in heaven" (119.89). Encyclopaedias have to undergo constant revision as knowledge increases and old ideas are discarded. But the Bible remains the same. So often people have jeered at its historical claims only to discover its astonishing accuracy. Historians once believed that the last king of Babylon was Nabonidus, not Belshazzar his son, as claimed in Daniel 5; but the unearthing in 1853 of a cylinder indicating that father and son acted as co-regents solved the problem. Hence the offer to make Daniel "third ruler" in the kingdom (Dan 5.16). Scientific precision is seen in the astounding paralleling of stars and grains of sand (Gen 15.5; 22.17), for Hipparchus the father of Greek astronomy could count only 1080 stars. Today, no longer restricted by the naked eye, we know that as far as men are concerned they are innumerable. So did Jeremiah (33.22)! Prophetic accuracy is seen in the detailed fulfilment of 300 predictions about the first coming of the Lord Jesus. His birth place (Mic 5.2), betrayal (Psa 41.9), unbroken bones despite crucifixion (Psa 34.20) and honourable burial (Isa 53.9) were all announced in advance. Of course, to say that the Bible is infallible does *not* mean it contains no errors. In its infallible unfolding of God's message to man, it truthfully records men's mistakes (John 10.20) and Satan's lies (for example, Genesis 3.4). But whether it speaks about salvation or creation or science or geography or history "Thy word is truth" (John 17.17), for our God "cannot lie" (Titus 1.2).

Then consider its **integrity**. This book pulls no punches. Paul tells us it is good for "reproof, correction, instruction" (2 Tim 3.16), for it rests on the premise that men are wrong and need putting right. It is in this sense the most honest book in the world. Thus, in no uncertain terms it tells me that I am alienated from God (Eph 4.18), blinded by Satan (2 Cor 4.4) and fundamentally corrupt (Psa 14.1-3). But what antagonises men is yet another testimony to its divine origin for, as a great Bible teacher once wrote, the Bible "is not such a book as man would write if he *could*, or could write if he *would*". Quite so. Someone else has said, "Show me a man who objects to the Bible and I'll show you a man who is doing something the Bible condemns". You see, God's word is not concerned to make us feel good about ourselves – rather, its frank, cutting edge pierces the conscience (Acts 2.37; 7.54).

But notice again its **universality**. Moslems say that the Koran (which preserves the religion and culture of the 7th century Arab world) cannot be translated out of Arabic without losing its essential power, but the Bible is trans-cultural and communicates in all languages. It is for old and young, Jew and Gentile (Rom 3.29), male and female (Gal 3.28), with its message about a universal Creator (Gen 1.1), universal corruption (Rom 5.12), and a universal cure (Acts 4.12). Further, it is marked by **simplicity**. Written not for some priestly caste but for ordinary folk, it uses plain words and adheres to the normal rules of language. That's why the very young can read and respond to it: "from a child [newborn child or infant]" Timothy had known the scriptures (2 Tim 3.15). Yet its truth ultimately surpasses the grasp of the greatest intellect. The new believer has his soul satisfied with the simple vocabulary of John's Gospel, while the mature saint finds his mind stretched to the limits by its profundity. It is not worldly wisdom but God's grace and simple faith that unlock the book (Matt 11.25; Psa 119.130).

Three great words to keep in mind are AUTHORITY (because the Bible is God's word it is to be believed and obeyed), INFALLIBILITY (because it is God's word it is without error), and SUFFICIENCY (because it is God's word it is all we need for life and godliness). When Paul left the Ephesians he commended them "to God, and to the word of his grace" (Acts 20.32) because that was enough. And it is enough for us too. No wonder the Lord Jesus tells us we have a firmer foundation for our faith than for our feet (Matt 24.35)! So keep reading, heeding and feeding on the word – it is our daily bread (Matt 4.4). Joseph Hart's advice is good:

> Say, Christian, would'st thou thrive,
> In knowledge of Thy Lord?
> Against no scripture ever strive,
> But tremble at His word.

> The Scriptures and the Lord
> Bear one tremendous name;
> The written and the Incarnate Word
> In all things are the same.

> The thoughts of men are lies;
> The word of God is true;
> To bow to *that* is to be wise:
> Then hear, and fear, and do.

Affectionately as always in Christ Jesus

WEEK EIGHTEEN

Letter No 18:

The Book of Revelation

As you left yesterday you mentioned the Book of Revelation. I wrote a few months back with a very brief survey of the Bible's basic teaching about the future, distinguishing between the Lord's return *for* His people (1 Thess 4.13-18) and His return *with* His people (Rev 19.11-21). But I'll try now to give you a simple way into this most tricky of Bible books. Indeed, it is the one New Testament book on which Calvin did *not* write a commentary. Tough it may be, but it is uniquely prefaced by a wonderful promise of blessing to all who read and keep it (Rev 1.3). The introduction also contains, from the lips of the Saviour Himself, a basic outline of the book as a whole (Rev 1.17-18):

> "I *am* he that liveth, and was dead; and, behold, I am alive for evermore, Amen; and have the keys of hell and of death. Write the things which thou hast seen, and the things which are, and the things which shall be hereafter".

It is, after all, "the Revelation [disclosure, unveiling] of Jesus Christ, which God gave unto him, to shew unto his servants things which must shortly come to pass" (Rev 1.1). Christ is therefore the centre and theme of the book. Fittingly He announces Himself to John as the One who went through death but came out in glorious resurrection triumph to live eternally, able to exercise authority over all things. Our Saviour holds the world in His hands! As a demonstration of His absolute authority He gives John an insight into future events, dividing His disclosure of truth into three sections: (i) **"the things which thou hast seen"** (which must mean the introductory vision of the risen Saviour in chapter 1); (ii) **"the things which are"** (which seems to relate to the seven letters to the churches in chapters 2 and 3, letters which effectively describe the entire age in which we now live); and (iii) **"the things which shall be hereafter [or better, 'the things which shall be after these things']"**, a phrase repeated in 4.1 ("after these things I saw") in order to introduce the final section of the book (4 – 22). So, (i) having first witnessed the glorified Christ, John then (ii) records His messages to seven representative local assemblies, before (iii) being taken up (4.1) to see a marvellous scene in heaven. Chapters 4 and 5 are a spectacular account of the worship of heaven, with Christ, "the Lamb as it had been slain", the centre of attention. The imagery of the lamb ties Revelation into the rest of the scriptures, echoing the language of Genesis, Exodus and John. Spend a while reading carefully through these verses as they will lift your heart in adoration:

> "And Isaac spake unto Abraham his father, and said, My father: and he said, Here *am* I, my son. And he said, Behold the fire and the wood: but where *is* the lamb for a burnt offering? And Abraham said, My son, God will provide himself a lamb for a burnt offering: so they went both of them together" (Gen 22.7-8).

> "Your lamb shall be without blemish, a male of the first year: ye shall take *it* out from the sheep, or from the goats: And ye shall keep it up until the fourteenth day of the same month: and the whole assembly of the congregation of Israel shall kill it in the evening" (Exo 12.5-6).

> "John seeth Jesus coming unto him, and saith, Behold the Lamb of God, which taketh away the sin of the world" (John 1.29).

The Lamb opens the seals of a scroll (possibly the title deeds of the earth), signalling the inauguration of divine judgment upon a world which has rejected all God's overtures of mercy. The major portion of the book goes on to describe in fearful detail the events which will come upon the earth as the same Person who laid down His life for us proceeds to execute God's judgment. It is worth noting that we as believers in the Lord Jesus belong to the second section of the book, in that we live in the current period of God's dealings with men, a period in which His anger is generally speaking held back while the gospel is preached. But one day, after we have been removed to glory (as recorded in 1 Thessalonians 4), God will declare war on the world which crucified His Son. One of the great comforts of reading this solemn book is to remember that "God hath not appointed us to wrath [which certainly includes the terrible wrath of this future period] but to obtain salvation by our Lord Jesus Christ, who died for us, that, whether we wake or sleep, we should live together with him" (1 Thess 5.9-10). In other words, Christians wait, not for the Great Tribulation (for Matthew 24.21 refers to the period covered in Revelation 6 - 19), but for the Lord Jesus Himself. It is always good to remember what we have been saved from (judgment) and what we have been saved for (glory), by God's grace.

You will find that the judgments (which are grouped under seals, trumpets and vials) increase as the book goes on, so that the earth's population is almost halved. Yet, despite all these clearly supernatural disasters, people will *not* repent and turn to the Lord (Rev 16.9-11) – demonstrating that miracles alone never save anybody. Rather, the Lord has to open our hearts to Himself by His grace. The grand climax is the Lord's public and visible return to the earth, accompanied by the armies of heaven. Read chapter 19 and see the folly of men who mobilize the United Nations to oppose the Creator's intervention! Having touched down on planet earth the Lord Jesus judges His remaining enemies, and then establishes His 1000-year kingdom (Rev 20.1-6) in fulfilment of Old Testament prophecy (Isa 2.1-5; 9.7; 32.1-2; Jer 23.3-8; 33.14-16; Dan 2.44; 7.13-14). During that time Satan will be chained and no longer able to trouble the world, which will for the first time in its history be governed righteously. Thereafter God allows a rebellion which ends in the current universe being burned up with fire (2 Pet 3.10-14; Rev 20.9-10), followed by the resurrection and judgment of the unsaved dead (Rev 20.11-15), and finally a new heaven and earth (Rev 21.1). You see, this book appropriately closes the entire canon of scripture because it declares the inevitable triumph of God's purpose to glorify Himself in Christ (Rev 15.18). Neither demons nor men can thwart His programme. In the very world which rejected Him, the Lord Jesus will reign. And in case the graphic details of the book have filled us with terror or anxiety, it finishes with a lovely guarantee of the Saviour's soon coming for *us*:

> "He which testifieth these things saith, Surely I come quickly.
> Amen. Even so, come, Lord Jesus" (Rev 22.20).

Note the earnest response of John to the Lord's promise. That's the best way to read the Bible: let its message fertilize your prayer life. God reveals the future not to pander to our idle curiosity but to stimulate our love for and obedience to Him in the present. As the old paint advert said, "before you start, think of the finish!" And we know where we are heading, because God has made it known to us.

Well, only a whistle stop tour of Revelation, I fear. If you want a fuller introduction to the book, Charles Ryrie's little Moody commentary is probably the simplest.

Affectionately as always in Christ Jesus

WEEK NINETEEN

Letter No 19:

Assembly Fellowship

Since your baptism is, God willing, coming up this weekend I thought I'd drop you a brief line on the seriousness of what you propose doing, in entering into assembly fellowship. Of course, I hope to be with you on Sunday, but in case something goes wrong I'd like to outline some of the privileges and responsibilities involved. Joining yourself to a company of Christians is not like becoming the member of a social club or a man-made society – rather, it is a solemn association with those who have been bonded together by the Lord Jesus Christ. Let me suggest that there are five great truths to bear in mind.

First, there is **commitment**. Like everything else in the Christian life, entering the fellowship of saints in a local church is a conscious, intelligent decision. The Lord's people are never to act thoughtlessly. Just as you trusted the Saviour with your eyes open to what was involved, so you join a church with the same awareness and determination. God does not desire His people to be alone – indeed we cannot manage alone – therefore He has provided us with a sphere of encouragement and exercise in which we can grow spiritually. In joining a company of saints I am declaring that this will be my spiritual home, and that I will make every effort to be at the gatherings. Indeed, it means arranging my life's timetable around the assembly, because the assembly is "the house of God" (1 Tim 3.15), where the Lord Jesus guarantees His presence however feeble the company numerically (Matt 18.20). If I am committed to the assembly where God has placed me I am not open to other offers. The behaviour of the apostles in Acts 4 sets the pattern. Having been threatened by the religious authorities, what did they do? "Being let go, they went to their own company, and reported all that the chief priests and elders had said unto them" (Acts 4.23). Note: "they went to *their own company*". There was a group of people to whom they belonged, and to whom they instinctively turned for support and encouragement. Saul's experience in Acts 9 is another good example. After his conversion we read, "Then was Saul certain days with the disciples which were at Damascus" (Acts 9.19). The little preposition "with" is ironically eloquent – Saul was enjoying fellowship with the very people he originally came to arrest. Further, when he later arrived in Jerusalem he had to work hard to convince the believers there that he really was a saved man (9.26-28), but that did not discourage him. Rather, in response to his persistence God raised up a man to testify to his genuine transformation. Thereafter he fully identified himself with the Jerusalem believers in all their activities.

Closely related to commitment is **continuance**. Those early believers "continued steadfastly" (Acts 2.42), regularly meeting together for Bible teaching ("the apostles' doctrine"), fellowship (sharing together in the service of God), the breaking of bread (remembering the Saviour in the special way He appointed at the Lord's Supper), and corporate prayers. Now we cannot do those things on our own: they are corporate exercises. And what we start we should continue. After all, that is the character of our God: "he which hath begun a good work in you will perform *it* until the day of Jesus Christ" (Phil 1.6). Alas, some people flit from company to company like butterflies, never settling down, never truly bringing anything to the assembly because they are simply not there long enough. Sticking at it through thick and thin is one of the evidences of God's grace in our lives. Ruth knew that travelling to Israel with her mother-in-law Naomi would not guarantee an easy time, but she went, prepared to continue come what may:

> "And Ruth said, Intreat me not to leave thee, *or* to return from following after thee: for whither thou goest, I will go; and where thou lodgest, I will lodge: thy people *shall be* my people, and thy God my God: Where thou diest, will I die, and there will I be buried: the LORD do so to me, and more also, *if ought* but death part thee and me. When she saw that she was stedfastly minded to go with her, then she left speaking unto her" (Ruth 1.16-18).

Then there is the **conduct** expected of those who love the Lord. Precisely because a local assembly is God's dwelling place it must reflect the character of its Owner and Occupier. That is why Paul instructs Timothy on "how thou oughtest to behave thyself in the house of God" (1 Tim 3.15). The Old Testament teaches us that "holiness becometh thine house, O LORD, for ever" (Psa 93.5). Therefore my life must accurately and worthily represent the holy God to whom I belong and the holy company in which He has placed me. As you read through the New Testament you will see that believers, being only fallible, sinful people like you and me, sometimes had to be disciplined. Of course, God is constantly disciplining us through the teaching of His word (Heb 12.5-11; 2 Tim 3.16-17), daily bringing us into line with His desires for us. But gross public sin has to be dealt with by the assembly. Read the solemn teaching of 1 Corinthians 5 (where a professing believer was guilty of serious immorality and had to be put out of the company). You see, the local church is like a holy temple for God's glory:

> "Know ye not that ye are the temple of God, and *that* the Spirit of God dwelleth in you? If any man defile the temple of God, him shall God destroy; for the temple of God is holy, which *temple* ye are" (1 Cor 3.16-17).

Such disciplinary action does not compromise a man's salvation, for that is eternally secure, but it safeguards the local assembly's holiness.

Fourth is **contribution**. Because I am in fellowship I am therefore expected to "share" (which is what fellowship means) in the expenses and activities of the work. The building costs money to maintain, there may be elderly and impoverished saints to support, there will be spiritual exercises of prayer, preaching and witness in which to engage. 1 Timothy 2.8 ("I will therefore that the men pray every where, lifting up holy hands, without wrath and doubting") makes clear that the males are entrusted by God with the responsibility of public prayer and worship. That means me! As you grow in grace you will find you want to take part vocally in the gatherings for prayer and praise. Since a New Testament assembly does not pay a clergyman to do the work, all the saints have a vital function to perform. There can be no sleeping partners.

Finally there is mutual **care**. Of course, we gather to the Lord first of all, but we also have a real care for each other. "Love to all the saints" (Col 1.4) is one of the outward evidences of genuine faith in Christ. For example, the believers at Damascus and Jerusalem showed practical love for Paul by arranging his safe escape from danger (Acts 9.23-25,29-30). You have already experienced the love of the saints at Coatbridge. It is so sad to hear people say they no longer attend a church because they "do not get anything out of it". But Hebrews 10.24-5 emphasises not what I get out but what I put into the gatherings. Come with a heart for God and you will never be disappointed.

Affectionately as always in Christ Jesus

Letter No 20:

The Lord's Supper

By the time you read this letter, you will, I trust, have been well and truly baptised. Of course, as you know, baptism in itself does nothing to you save make you wet: that is to say, it merely pictures what God in grace did for you the moment you trusted His Son. But it *is* a great public demonstration of your faith in the Lord Jesus Christ, an opportunity to testify to what He has done for your soul, and the first step of obedience on the Christian pathway. Of course, to do what the Lord says does not mean you will have some spectacular vision of angels or even a deep spiritual thrill, but it gives us the assurance that we have pleased our Master. After all, the Lord Jesus said, "if you love me, keep my commandments" (John 14.15), and "if ye know these things, happy are ye if you do them" (John 13.17). Notice that clear recipe for happiness. What we know from the word of God we should do – and that guarantees blessing. There may be no recognition or acclaim down here, but to do the Saviour's will is the greatest privilege on earth.

You will by now already have attended your first breaking of bread meeting as an observer. Perhaps it will not be amiss if I try to draw attention to some of the characteristics of that gathering, if only because it is so different from what people expect. For a start, it is *not* a meeting for teaching the Bible, or praying for our needs, or preaching to the unsaved. It is not even primarily for mutual fellowship. It is for worship. In Old Testament times Israel was given an entire calendar of annual worship feasts to observe, to remind them of everything that God had done and was going to do for them. You can read about this in Leviticus 23. For example, the Passover was a remembrance of their wonderful deliverance from Egyptian slavery; but, unknown to them at the time, it also pointed forward to our much greater deliverance from bondage to sin. Now, the

Lord Jesus has not given His people today any annual feasts. Christmas and Easter have no real basis in the word of God. Rather, we have a regular corporate remembrance whereby a local assembly gathers specifically to focus attention upon the person who means most to us.

What is the Lord's Supper? Biblical titles provide much instruction. It is called "the Lord's Supper" (1 Cor 11.20). The context here is human failure, but God draws blessing out of error by using it as an occasion for teaching truth. This title underlines the authority of the gathering, because the supper is the Lord's, not ours. Since He is Lord (a title of deity and dignity) we should make every endeavour to come on time in a spirit of reverence and holy intelligence. The spiritual condition of every believer is vital to the gathering. Secondly it speaks of affection, because in the Middle East supper was the chief meal of the day, a time of rest, refreshment, and family reunion. In other words, this gathering is a time of loving fellowship with the Lord – there is to be nothing mechanical or perfunctory about it. Third, it suggests assurance, for at the Lord's Supper we can guarantee the presence of the host Himself (Matt 18.20). The "breaking of bread" (Acts 2.42; 20.7) describes what we do. In other words it is a simple meal. Indeed, the phrase is often used in a purely secular context (Acts 2.46; 27.35; Luke 24.30,35). You see, what the Saviour asked His people to do was available to all, however poor they might be, because it involved no costly trappings, no ornate ceremony, no impressive building, no professional clergy. All they needed was a loaf of bread and a cup of wine. Simple indeed, but by no means insignificant for both the bread and the contents of the cup speak to us of the Lord Jesus. They picture His death (for blood separated from the body inevitably means loss of life), His suffering (for bread is produced by grinding, wine by crushing), and the blessing which we enjoy in Him (Psa 104.15). They are only symbols of a work complete and unrepeatable, a work we have come into the good of because we are not asked to look at, hold or analyse the bread and wine but take and eat/drink. What a marvellous illustration of enjoying the practical benefits of Calvary!

Why do we do it? Well, because the Lord says so (Luke 22.19) – and that is enough! His command is recorded historically in the gospels and repeated in Paul's special exposition of the Supper (1 Cor 11.23-34). Therefore we do it "in remembrance of me" (1 Cor 11.23-24), for our great and inexhaustible theme is the Lord Jesus Himself in all the fullness of His person and work, with special emphasis upon His atoning death (which we "show" or "proclaim", 1 Cor 11.26). So the gathering is for Him and all about Him. This means that all our hymns, prayers, and readings are to focus upon Him.

Where do we do it? Since we read that the early disciples broke bread in Jerusalem (Acts 2.42), at Troas (20.7) and in Corinth (1 Cor 11) it is safe to say that it is done on earth! That is, it is not for heaven but for now. *Then* we shall see the Lord Jesus as He is; *now* we just have the symbols. Further, in the Bible it is always connected with the fellowship and discipline of the local assembly – Paul places it squarely in the context of saints coming together "in the church" (1 Cor 11.18). This of course is the letter in which he writes solemnly about both individual responsibility (11.28 – I am to make sure that I know what I am doing as I remember the Lord) and corporate responsibility (1 Cor 5.13). There can never be anything casual, thoughtless, or automatic about remembering the Saviour. It is a holy privilege which I cannot take lightly.

Who is there? Pre-eminently the Lord is there. Paul received his instruction "from the Lord", yet he was not in the Upper Room in the gospel accounts, for he was not even saved at that time. He got his teaching directly the Lord in heaven. And that risen Lord is where His people gather to His name (Matt 18.20; 1 Cor 14.25). Further, there are angelic observers present (read 1 Cor 11.10; Eph 3.10; 1 Pet 1.12) who cannot benefit from Calvary but who can learn something of God's grace from saved sinners like us. And all the believers in the local assembly should be there. Clearly in Acts 2.41-42 all those who received the word and were baptised continued steadfastly "in the apostles' doctrine and fellowship, and in breaking of bread, and in prayers". It is worth noting that that they did not simply turn up for the breaking of bread as though the other gatherings (for teaching and prayer) were not important – no, they persisted in *all* features of assembly life.

When do we do it? We have no strict commands but just hints to which love will be quick to respond. It seems clear that the disciples at Troas met regularly on "the first day of the week" (our Sunday) to break bread (Acts 20.7). Although Paul was in a hurry to reach Jerusalem (20.16) he still waited there seven days so as to be able to join them for the Lord's Supper. After all, the first day of the week was (i) the resurrection day (John 20.1,19,26) which the Lord had set apart by His post-resurrection appearances, (ii) the day when the Holy Spirit had descended (Acts 2.1), and (iii) the day set aside for giving (1 Cor 16.2-3). So we remember Him on the first day of the week 'until he come' (1 Cor 11.26): it will be our weekly exercise for the whole of this age as we look for His coming to take us home. It keeps the mind alert and the heart aflame.

God willing, I shall write to you next about how to prepare for this gathering, for the way we spend our Saturday evening will affect the way we honour the Lord the following day. May the Lord fill your heart with an ever increasing appreciation of the immensity of His love for you.

Affectionately yours in Christ Jesus.

Letter No 21:

The Pilgrim's Progress (ii)

I thought I'd continue with a bit more *Pilgrim's Progress*. After all, if Bunyan could get away with a Part Two, why can't I? Last time I wrote along these lines you will recall that I introduced you to some of the people you may meet on the Christian pathway – folk who claim to be saved (and some of whom doubtless are) but who are not necessarily good patterns for the child of God. We need to choose our spiritual role models with due care. Let's look at some more. As I walked through the wilderness of this world I lighted upon a certain place where was an assembly, and there I laid me down – no, not to sleep, but to enjoy fellowship and engage in spiritual exercises with the saints of God.

In the course of your spiritual experience you may run into **Mr Hobby-Horse**. He can normally be recognised by his tendency, whether on the platform or in private conversation, always to harp upon the same topic. Unwilling to feed upon the amazing wealth and variety of teaching in God's word, he latches onto one doctrine or issue and makes that his constant theme. As a result, like someone wearing tinted spectacles, he colours everything in scripture with his obsession. I recall the story of a man who loved to find references to baptism everywhere. His long-suffering friends decided to drive him out of his groove by asking him to minister on an obscure verse in Revelation, thinking that, since there was no water in sight, he would at least have to address the contextual meaning of the scripture. Alas for their hopes! When he rose to preach he said, "Now this is a most interesting verse as it is one of the few in the Bible which does not deal with baptism. Speaking of baptism...", and off he was again on his usual track. Of course, this is often nothing more than a harmless fad. Indeed, some very gifted Bible teachers become associated with a particular line of truth (prophecy, assembly principles, creation) because they minister on it so frequently, although of course one hopes that they do so from passages which genuinely teach it. Nevertheless, it is well to remember that the apostle Paul never gained this reputation. Rather, he 'did not shrink from declaring...the whole counsel of God' (Acts 20.27). The teacher's curriculum is *all* God's word. Trouble with Mr Hobby-Horse is that he is a bit like his much more dangerous ancestor, Mr Stretch Scripture, who would wilfully twist the meaning of the word to suit his predilections. Peter refers to him and his kind in his second letter: "they that are unlearned and unstable wrest, as *they do* also the other scriptures, unto their own destruction" (2 Pet 3.16). Peter's word "wrest" (your Vine will show you that it is used only here) means literally to put on the rack. Just as a torturer can get his victim to say anything he wants, so such people wrench the scriptures to suit their fancy or conform to their doctrine. This is the practice of all the cults. Now we just cannot do this to God's word. It must be allowed to speak for itself, even though it disagree with our cherished preconceptions. "Let God be true and every man a liar". Nor should we really narrow ourselves to pet topics, although I suppose we all tend to return to our favourite passages. It is impossible to subsist effectively on a "Handel's Greatest Hits" selection from scripture. One of the great benefits of regularly reading through the Bible each year is that it ensures we enjoy a balanced diet of the whole word of God. After all, the Lord Jesus told us that we live "by every word which proceedeth out of the mouth of God" (Matt 4.4). Keep on getting the whole of the word into your heart, and you will be more than adequately nourished spiritually.

One of the sadder encounters of the Christian life is with **Mr and Mrs Grouser** and their family. You only get to know what these people are really like when you are in their home, as their public surface is usually polite and orthodox. Only in private will they fully release their bitter grievances with the assembly, with the elders, with the meetings, with the saints. I remember bumping into such a family many years ago. Almost before I had taken a seat in their house I was being served with a formidable supper of cakes and criticism. Their disaffection with the local assembly was all too obvious. After a while I began to wonder why they bothered to remain in fellowship at all. And within a few years, not surprisingly, they left. Now, all local assemblies (indeed, all companies of believers) have problems – which is only to be expected as saints and elders are merely saved sinners. You know as well as I do the capacity for evil within our hearts. But we must differentiate between the unfortunate failures of the Lord's people in a local church (failures to live up to the high standard of God's word) and the biblical foundation on which the assembly is built.

The first can be dealt with biblically. Indeed, every teaching meeting is designed to bring our lives into line with the truth. And those who grumble about the apathy and unspirituality of the saints may well find, if they look honestly within, that they are themselves of like passions. None of us has anything to boast about. The remedy is not to grouse but to put one's back into the work of the Lord in accordance with Hebrews 10.23-25:

> "Let us hold fast the profession of *our* faith without wavering; (for he *is* faithful that promised;) And let us consider one another to provoke unto love and to good works: Not forsaking the assembling of ourselves together, as the manner of some *is*; but exhorting *one another*: and so much the more, as ye see the day approaching".

In other words, we should encourage rather than discourage one another! Those, however, who wilfully resist the scriptural principles of the local assembly (especially the more unfashionable ones, such as the truth of headship, the simplicity of the Lord's Supper, the absence of a paid clergyman), and who insidiously whisper behind the scenes to stir up trouble and discontent, cannot be tolerated. Such conduct is despicable. You see, when I enter the fellowship of a local assembly I am not only received by the assembly but I simultaneously identify myself with all it stands for. Let us never become fault-finders but rather, always remembering our own failures, seek, by God's grace, to be a positive help.

But there are also some lovely people on the journey. Just to meet them is to refresh the soul. The winning answer to a "What is the quickest way to London" competition was only two words: "good company". And in a local assembly we are travelling together to heaven in good company. You will, I am sure, meet **Mr and Mrs Stickability**. Every assembly has at least one such couple. They are usually elderly, having been on the pathway for many years, and are still going strong despite discouragement and disappointment. Unlike the Grousers, their home is one where the scriptures rather than the failings of the saints are talked about. They have put much into the company over the years (although they themselves will probably not tell you that – others will), they have continued steadfastly in good times and bad, they have taken up a work (perhaps in the Sunday School, perhaps in tracting an area, perhaps in showing hospitality to visitors) and stuck with it even though they have received little thanks. Of course, what they do they do primarily for the Lord, not for men. Trace the references to Aquila and Priscilla in the New Testament and you will find that not only are they constantly mentioned together (an example of godly marriage), they minister together to the Lord's people (for example, providing accommodation for Paul, and later for a whole assembly). The Bible, you see, not only gives warnings of behaviour to avoid – it also furnishes examples of godly people we can safely imitate. Of such the instruction is, "whose faith follow" (Heb 13.7). Well, even single men can learn from these examples. As someone said to me long ago, reliability is far more important than ability. It does not matter how spiritually gifted you are if you do not attend the meetings, if you cannot be counted upon to pull your weight. I cannot think of a higher commendation than that which the Lord Jesus gave to a woman who expressed her devotion to Him in a quiet but costly way: "she hath done what she could" (Mark 14.8). The Lord expects no more (and no less) than that. May we both try, with His gracious help, to be faithful, trustworthy, steady members of the local assembly in which He has placed us.

Affectionately as ever in Christ Jesus

WEEK TWENTY TWO

Letter No 22:

Preparing for the Lord's Supper (i)

I promised to write and suggest ways in which we can prepare effectively for the Lord's Supper since this is the meeting of the local church in which every believer, young or old, male or female, has a special responsibility. It is the gathering in which we all physically take part in a symbolic activity which illustrates pointedly what the Saviour has done for us.

The first thing to keep in mind is the prime **purpose** of the gathering. Once we have that clear we shall not be sidetracked. The Lord's words are plain enough:

> "And he took bread, and gave thanks, and brake *it*, and gave unto them, saying, This is my body which is given for you: this do in remembrance of me. Likewise also the cup after supper, saying, This cup *is* the new testament in my blood, which is shed for you" (Luke 22.19-20).

What we do is for a remembrance of Christ Jesus. The gathering thus aims to honour, to exalt, to magnify Him. So it is not a matter of coming together to listen to a gifted teacher of the word (as in Acts 11.26), or to pour out our heart's supplications before God (as in Acts 4.23-31), or even to enjoy fellowship with the saints (as in Acts 20.11, where the Troas believers broke bread and ate in a shared social meal after the spiritual exercises earlier in the evening). Now all those activities are precious and essential aspects of assembly life. Nevertheless the Lord's Supper stands apart because it is uniquely for the Lord's glory rather than for our good. This is what worship is all about – it concentrates, not upon me, my needs, my failings, or even my blessings, but upon what God is in Himself. We live in a self-centred, self-obsessed, self-occupied world; but we have been saved to be occupied with Christ. Like the disciples on the mount of transfiguration, we love to see "no man save Jesus only" (Matt 17.8). This knowledge will therefore inform everything we do at the Supper. The hymns I give out will be chosen not because they are my personal favourites but because they cast the spotlight upon Christ. The prayers I utter will not be about my individual needs but about God's beloved Son, designed to encourage the Lord's people in their remembrance. Any readings from scripture will be for the purpose of directing the attention of the saints to the excellences of Christ Jesus. Whatever you do, always ask yourself, "Will my contribution to the gathering focus the saints' minds on the Lord or will it distract them?"

That settled, the next thing is to set aside regular time for **preparation**. Worship cannot be switched on at will, like an electric light. There is a lovely illustration in Deuteronomy. Remember the setting: the nation of Israel had been rescued from Egyptian slavery, led through the desert and was now about to be brought into Canaan. Once the Israelite arrived safely in the land, he must bring his token of gratitude to Jehovah (Deut 26.1-11). He was to take of the first fruits of the land, put them in a basket, take them to God's gathering centre and offer them before the Lord. This would be a clear testimony to the fact that he was right now in the practical enjoyment of God's goodness (vv.1-2), for all those fruits came from the Lord in the first place. Only God's redeemed people (those who have been delivered from bondage and brought into salvation) can worship. You will notice that this command was addressed not the nation in general but to the individual ("thou"). Every assembly of God's people is made up of individuals each of whom is responsible for a personal exercise of heart in spiritual matters. I cannot sit back and rely on others to do what I should do. More, he was given detailed instructions: "take... bring...put...go...say" (vv.2-3). Worship is not a free for all: it must be offered in accordance with divine rules (note the "must" in John 4.24), not human whims. Again, it involves lowliness of heart (v.5): just as each Israelite had nothing in which to boast, being a son of Jacob the deceiver ("a Syrian ready to perish"), so we are merely children of sinful Adam (Rom 5.19), saved by God's sovereign grace alone. Therefore the Israelite's confession as he handed over his basket of produce (vv.7-9) was a glad testimony to a God who had taken the initiative, who "heard... looked...brought us forth...brought us into...gave". As we meet to remember the Saviour we are acknowledging that all the glory in salvation is His. But here's the crucial point – the Israelite had to take time in advance to select his produce (and first fruits implies the best), place it in his basket and take it to the priest. This he would have to do at home. Similarly, our preparation for the Lord's Supper will be done before ever we reach the meeting place. It may sometimes be better to stay at home and study the word on a Saturday evening rather than travel around to a lot of outside meetings. Going to bed late is no way to be fresh for the Lord's Day morning. My first responsibility is always to the local assembly in which God has placed me. There I *must* pull my weight.

Now the instructions in Deuteronomy establish an important principle. Sinful creatures have nothing in themselves to offer a holy God who can only accept perfection. Therefore, just as the Israelite chose from the various fruits of the land in order to give back to God what God had first given him (Deut 26.10), so we offer to the Father our feeble appreciation of the One He gave us. In practice that means that I turn to the word of God for information about the glories of the Lord so that I can mention them to God. Indeed, the word is our only authoritative source of information about Christ. The gospels are obviously full of Him, but don't overlook Old Testament **predictions**. Try Genesis 49.10,24 (look for Shiloh, the stone, and the shepherd), Deuteronomy 18.18-19 (the prophet like Moses), 2 Sam 7.12-16 (the descendant of David), Isaiah 7.14 (Immanuel); 9.6-7; 42.1-4 (the perfect servant); 53 (the sacrifice).

But there are more than just prophecies; there are **pictures**. Read Genesis 22, where Abraham is told to offer up his beloved son Isaac as a burnt offering to God. Now, let's see what we can learn that might stimulate our worship. First, Abraham and Isaac ascending the mountain together (Gen 22.6) remind us of the perfect fellowship between Father and Son in our salvation: "He spared not his own Son, but delivered him up for us all" (Rom 8.32). Second, the submissiveness of Isaac (he seems not to have resisted his aged father) anticipates the voluntary obedience of the Son unto death: "Therefore doth my Father love me, because I lay down my life, that I might take it again" (John 10.17; Phil 2.8). Third, Abraham's confidence that God would provide Himself a lamb (22.8) of course looks forward to John Baptist's announcement in John 1.29. Fourth, the miraculous supply of a last-minute ram substitute for Isaac (22.13) makes us think of the Saviour as our substitute on Calvary – we deserved to die, but He "suffered for sins, the just for the unjust" (1 Pet 3.18). Fifth, since the Angel of the Lord (as so often in the Old Testament) seems to be a pre-incarnate appearance of the Son of God, He who intervened to stay Abraham's hand (22.11-12) was the same One who would Himself endure the suffering of the cross, receiving from God all the punishment that was our due. Finally, the sacrifice was a "burnt offering", where the emphasis fell primarily on delighting God's heart rather than dealing with sin. You will see this if you study the details about the different offerings in the first few chapters of Leviticus. The death of Christ was to God "a sweet-smelling savour" (Eph 5.2). Just to meditate on these Old Testament types of Calvary is to fill our minds with thoughts of the Saviour – and such thoughts we can, with the Holy Spirit's aid, offer to God when we gather with the saints. I said earlier that the Lord's Supper is all for the Lord – but, marvellous to tell, one of its by-products is that it does *us* good because it concentrates our heart's affections upon the most wonderful person in the universe. There can be nothing better than that.

Affectionately yours in Christ Jesus

WEEK TWENTY THREE

Letter No 23:

Secular Employment

Since a number of ex-students have recently been requesting references, and since I know you are thinking about your future, I thought I'd take the opportunity to jot down a few notes on the biblical principles relating to secular employment.

First, **why** should we work? It is very clear that the Lord's people are never to be parasites. Writes Paul, "even when we were with you, this we commanded you, that if any would not work, neither should he eat" (2 Thess 3.10). This principle is evident from the Garden of Eden onwards. From the time of the Fall, man was given by God the serious responsibility to work for his living in a world damaged by the results of his own sin (Gen 3.17-19), work which would often be physically and mentally wearisome. There are benefits in this: it is a valuable reminder that we live on a ruined planet, yet simultaneously a preservative from much of the wickedness in which we would doubtless indulge had we the opportunity. Too much free time can be perilous. But work is not merely a consequence of sin. Even in a world of unsullied innocence Adam was given a task: "God took the man, and put him into the garden of Eden to dress it [translated "till" in Gen 2.5 and 3.23, and elsewhere often by "serve"] and to keep it [guard, maintain, preserve]" (Gen 2.15). So God always gives His creatures duties to perform. And we have been created in such a way that there is a deep satisfaction in doing our work well (Eccles 5.18). That is why unemployed men speedily become demoralized. Even the Son of God laboured while He was on the earth, being known to His neighbours as "the carpenter" (Mark 6.3). It is worth underlining the point, though, that we work primarily to meet our basic needs, not to make vast amounts of money (1 Tim 6.6-8). The dangers of the latter are clearly exposed in 1 Timothy 6.9-10. The amassing of material wealth is ultimately pointless for those who are only down here for a few years, and whose real riches are in heaven, whither by grace they are bound (Matt 6.19-21). We work, therefore, to keep ourselves and our family dependents, and to avoid being chargeable to others. The apostle Paul, who had the right to be supported by the believers among whom he laboured spiritually (1 Cor 9.1-14), frequently worked with his own hands (1 Cor 4.12). I sometimes hear people say that he was only driven into this expedient because he was not receiving the practical aid from Christians to which he was entitled, but Paul does not seem to offer this as a reason. Rather, he presents himself as an example for all saints of the blessedness of giving rather than taking (Acts 20.33-35; 1 Thess 2.9; 2 Thess 3.7-9). Indeed, in the same passage that he establishes his right to be supported, he tells us that he deliberately waived that right (1 Cor 9.15-23). Thus, when he visited Corinth, he stayed with a couple who, like himself, were tentmakers, and worked (Acts 18.1-3). The Bible thus makes plain the dignity of work. Further, combining secular labour with spiritual makes for an ideal balance: that is, it gives us legitimate daily contact with unsaved people so that we can show them Christ's love in the workplace, it provides us with real situations in which the teachings of the word can be put into practice, and it prevents us from ever growing tired of studying the scriptures. We return home after a hard day's toil to find refreshment and stimulus in the scriptures and the gatherings of the saints. My advice to young men who want to serve the Lord is this: seek to find (in God's goodness) work which will allow you the time to be a help in your local assembly. You will then have the privilege of serving the saints while supporting yourself with secular employment.

But that leads to the question, **where** should we work? Well, the Bible does not tell us exactly what each of us should be doing any more than it names the girl we should marry or the town in which we should live. Rather, it lays down basic principles to keep in mind. First, we should obviously not engage in secular work which requires disobedience to God's word. It would hardly be right for a believer to work in the gambling industry, or as the landlord of a public house, since both promote sinful activities. Second, we should seek employment which, as far as it is possible, will leave us free to fulfil our commitment to the local assembly in which God has placed us. Therefore work which keeps us away from the Lord's Supper and the activities of the Lord's Day is to be avoided. There are some spheres of employment which are particularly attractive to believers precisely because they appear to be humanitarian and altruistic. Medicine springs immediately to mind. But here we have to be especially careful because the good is often the enemy of the best. That is to say, the satisfaction of meeting the physical needs of our fellow men can become so all-consuming that it distracts us from the more important duty of obedience to God. Someone usefully puts it like this: "disciples should not give priority to tasks that the unsaved can do just as well as Christians". Quite so. The unsaved can be just as efficient as ourselves in many spheres – what they *cannot* do is give God His due in worship and service. The things of God are always to be our priority. Occasionally therefore the thoughtful believer will refuse promotion because it would involve such a demand upon his time and energies that his spiritual life and his assembly responsibility would suffer. Does he therefore miss out? Never forget the Lord's own promise: "them that honour me I will honour, and they that despise me shall be lightly esteemed" (1 Sam 2.30). In other words, earthly loss can be heavenly gain. The second and third man on this earth chose rather different but understandable trades: Cain was a "tiller of the ground" while Abel was a "keeper of sheep" (Gen 4.2). Nothing wrong with either, one would say. But interestingly Abel's work allowed him to give to God the offering He desired – not the fruits of a cursed ground but a blood sacrifice. Back in Genesis 3.21 God Himself had provided Adam and Eve with a suitable covering which necessitated an animal death and thereby established a principle which continues throughout the scriptures, that "without shedding of blood is no remission [of sin]" (Heb 9.22). I wonder if Abel had learned from this and chosen his career accordingly.

Finally, **how** should we work? Scripture is clear that believers are to do their best in all they do because this is a part of their testimony. A good many of the Saviour's parables involve the workplace, and uphold the importance of diligence, faithfulness, and probity. Paul addresses believing slaves (men who had obviously not opted for such a position but who found themselves in it by force of circumstance) thus: "whatsoever ye do, do *it* heartily, as to the Lord, and not unto men; Knowing that of the Lord ye shall receive the reward of the inheritance: for ye serve the Lord Christ" (Col 3.22-25). Notice the astonishing assertion at the close – converted slaves (by no means regarded highly in Roman society) were the *Lord's* servants! When Joseph was sold into slavery and became first of all a servant in Potiphar's house and later (because of false accusation) a prisoner, he did not give way to bitter resentment but rather worked hard and well (Gen 39.1-6,20-23). In the adverse circumstances in which he found himself (circumstances, of course, overruled by God) he did his very best. And that is our pattern.

My father left school with little formal education and became a poorly paid machine operator in a hosiery factory. When that suddenly closed he had to find work in a builder's merchants. His work was neither glamorous nor well rewarded, but I never heard him complain, and he faithfully supported his family until the Lord took him home. More important, he was an active worker in his local assembly as an elder, superintendent of the Sunday School, leader of the weekly Old Folk's Home evangelistic meeting, and the Hospital Party. When I become a bit disgruntled with my work, I think of my dad. He accomplished far more spiritually than I ever shall.

Well – there are just a few thoughts for you to bear in mind. May the Lord guide you in His grace so that you find the employment of His choosing, for His glory and your blessing.

Affectionately as always in Christ Jesus

Letter No 24:

Preparing for the Lord's Supper (ii)

Last Thursday, a mutual friend spoke at Eastpark about the practical value of preparing for the breaking of bread meeting. He was really very good – I must get a recording of the message for you. One of the points that struck me was this: thinking about a coming Lord's Day gives a real focus to our regular Bible reading. As we read the word we can be garnering information about Christ for use in our offering. So here goes with more suggestions about how best to prepare for this very special gathering of God's people.

In my earlier letter I mentioned the fact that the Lord Jesus is the theme of the Old Testament as well as the New. But of course He is obviously central to the gospel narratives. So here are seven ways in which you can scour the gospels for truth about Him which will both feed your soul and provide thoughts for worship. Always have a notebook and pen handy so you can jot down what you are learning and enjoying. First, be alert to the way in which the gospels record the **fulfilment of Old Testament prophecy**. This is the special theme of Matthew (with its key phrase, "that it might be fulfilled") although it is a common factor in the other three accounts as well. In the first few chapters of Matthew we meet the Lord as the virgin born Immanuel (Matt 1.22-23), Israel's promised ruler (2.5-6), God's own Son (2.15), a Nazarene (2.23), and one whose ministry would specially benefit those on the borders of the Promised Land (4.14-16). That last quotation, referring to "Galilee of the Gentiles", is particularly encouraging for folk like us who are non-Jews. God's dear Son came not just to His own people Israel but to bring eternal benefit to those outside (Rom 15.8-12). God had long in advance through the scriptures prepared His chosen nation for the arrival of His Son, and the Saviour came in precise implementation of every prophetic detail. It is marvellous to see how apparent contradictions were resolved: He could truthfully be said to come from Bethlehem, Egypt and Nazareth. God's word cannot fail (Isa 55.11).

Second, consider the Saviour's **names and titles**. Bible names are usually of great import, often revealing something of the personality of the bearer. Just remember that *name indicates nature*. Thus Adam means "red earth" (the raw material of his body), Isaac means "laughter" (recalling Abraham's unbelieving chuckle at the announcement that he would be a father), Judah means "praise" (what that tribe and the nation as a whole were meant to bring to God). But the "Lord Jesus Christ" overflows with significance – and He uniquely lived up to His names. "Lord" indicates both deity (echoing the Old Testament name of God) and authority; the name Jesus ("Jehovah saves", explained in Matthew 1.21) testifies to His deity, humanity and saving ministry; while the official designation "Christ" (the Greek equivalent of the Hebrew "Messiah", meaning "the anointed person") alludes to His great offices as prophet (to reveal what God is like), priest (to deal with sin), and king (to reign over the earth). You can check the Old Testament evidence in 1 Kings 19.16 (which deals with both prophets and kings), and Leviticus 8.30. In Matthew 1.1 the Lord Jesus is introduced as son of David (fulfilling God's regal promises in 2 Samuel 7.12-16) and son of Abraham (answering God's covenant with Abraham in Genesis 22.18 that one of his descendants would bring blessing to the whole earth). Again, in Matthew He is called son of God (Matt 3.17) and son of man (8.20). The first indicates true deity, the second genuine manhood and more (Daniel 7.13-14 and Matthew 26.63-65 suggest how much more).

Third, investigate the **miracles**, all rich in teaching. Take the first in Matthew (8.2-4). This demonstrates His unfailing ability to meet men's needs, His loving willingness to intervene in response to a man's desperate plea, His practical tenderness in dealing with the individual (for He had no need to *touch* the leper at all – a mere word would have sufficed – yet He deliberately laid His hand on one who, because of the strict Jewish hygiene code, would not have experienced human contact for many years). But His concern for the leper is matched by His insistence that God's law be observed (hence His reference to the ceremony for the cleansing of the leper, which you can read about in Leviticus 14). The Lord always honoured the word. A fascinating study is the seven (or is it eight?) sign miracles in John's gospel, specifically selected to draw us to faith in Christ (John 20.30-31).

Fourth, the **parables** are another source of information about the Lord as so often we can glimpse aspects of Him in their storyline. For example, the tale of the two sons in Matthew 21.28-32 (picturing the hypocritical Pharisees and the repentant publicans) makes us think of another Son who was perfectly obedient to His Father's desires, even to the extent of death (John 14.31). The Good Samaritan (Luke 10.29-37) inevitably reminds us of Christ. Indeed, we can see contrasts and comparisons between the Samaritan and the Saviour. Unlike the Jericho road traveller, the Lord journeyed from heaven to earth, and paid the cost of salvation by His atoning death. But both were despised (John 8.48; Isa 53.3), both came right where the needy one was (Gal 4.4; John 6.33), both showed compassion (Luke 7.13), both stooped to rescue (Phil 2.6-8), both acted as deliverers (Luke 4.18), both paid a price (1 Pet 1.18-19), and both promised to return (John 14.3). Then again, the shepherd who found his sheep (Luke 15.3-7) obviously pictures our good shepherd (John 10.11).

Fifth, the Saviour's personal **claims** are worth close study. Try the seven great "I AM" statements in John, statements which combine an assertion of deity (for "I AM" echoes the name of God revealed to Moses in Exodus 3.13-14) with an assurance of sufficiency. Whatever our need, Christ can satisfy it. For the hungry, He is the bread of life; for the darkened, the light of the world; for outsiders, the door…but you can look them all up for yourself. That is the great joy of Bible study – individually digging out nuggets of truth to enjoy.

Sixth, the gospel records are full of remarkable **testimonies** to the identity of the Lord Jesus. God always makes sure that His Son is never left without witness to who He truly is. Consider, for example, in John 1 the words of John Baptist (1.26-34), Andrew (1.41), Philip (1.45) and Nathanael (1.49). But the grandest testimony of all is that of God the Father Himself. Take the words uttered on the mount of transfiguration: "This is my beloved Son, in whom I am well pleased; hear ye him" (Matt 17.5). One of the most encouraging things about this (as far as I am concerned) is that God, in speaking well of His Son, actually confines Himself to Old Testament language. Just as, when dealing with Satan in the desert (Matt 4.4), the Son restricted Himself to the same weapon which all His people can use, so too the Father shows that the written word is sufficient to inform our praise. Here are the allusions: "my son" (Psa 2.7), "beloved" (Gen 22.2), "well pleased" (Isa 42.1), "hear him" (Deut 18.15). Think them through.

Finally (one always has to stop at seven!) note the **unintentional commendations** spoken by enemies of the Lord who did not fully understand what they said. Pilate announced "Behold the man" (John 19.5) and unknowingly quoted Zechariah 6.12. But the Lord Jesus was indeed the only true, perfect man who has ever lived because He was everything that men ought to be. But look too at what the Jewish leaders said in their envy and mockery (Luke 15.2 and Matthew 27.42). We, of course, are profoundly thankful that He received poor sinners and "saved others". After all, He has received and saved us.

Again I have trespassed on your patience, but I hope you will have found a few hints here to stimulate your study and inform your adoration. You will discover as you continue to grow in grace that to be satisfied with Christ is the recipe for true contentment of soul. So keep on going!

Affectionately as always in Christ Jesus

WEEK TWENTY FIVE

Letter No 25:

Some Thoughts on Witness

As I have some time spare this afternoon and also because I know you are deeply concerned about your family and long to see them saved, I thought I'd try to jot down a few thoughts on the subject of witness. One of the sure signs of a work of grace in the soul is a desire that others be brought into similar blessing. Like the lepers who unexpectedly came upon the spoils of the scattered Syrian army we cannot keep the glad news to ourselves: "We do not well: this day *is* a day of good tidings, and we hold our peace" (2 Kings 7.9). As someone has said, "witnessing is simply one beggar telling other beggars where to find bread".

First of all let us establish the **mandate**. At the end of each Gospel narrative the Lord Jesus, on the eve of His ascension back into heaven, entrusted His disciples with the task of telling others about Him and His finished work. Each record has its distinctive emphasis. Matthew 28.18-20 foregrounds the teaching commission ("make disciples...baptize...teach"), for those who surrender to the claims of Christ are to be baptized and instructed in godly conduct. Conversion means conformity to the Lord's will. Mark 16.15 reveals the universal scope of a message ("preach the gospel to every creature") which spills out beyond the confines of Judaism, while Luke 24.45-49 details both its basic condition ("repentance") and the divine enablement provided for its preachers ("power from on high"). Feeble saints need special help to proclaim a word which goes against the grain of human nature. John 20.30-31 illustrates the commission at work in John's own explanation for his book: under the Spirit's guidance he has selected from the ministry of Christ so that his readers might come to believe in Him. Now of course in context all these directions relate to the immediate earthly followers of Christ – the twelve disciples and their associates. But the principle abides: those who have come into the good of God's great salvation are responsible to testify to His grace. This truth pervades both testaments. As the psalmist says: "O give thanks unto the LORD, for *he is* good: for his mercy *endureth* for ever. Let the redeemed of the LORD say *so*, whom he hath redeemed from the hand of the enemy" (Psa 107.2). And Paul urges the Philippians to be "blameless and harmless, the sons of God, without rebuke, in the midst of a crooked and perverse nation, among whom ye shine as lights in the world; holding forth the word of life" (Phil 2.15-16).

Second, what is our **motive**? Well, we do what the Lord says simply because the Lord says so, and in one sense there need be no other reason. As the Saviour asks, "why call ye me, Lord, Lord, and do not the things which I say?" (Luke 6.46) Yet obedience to the Lord Jesus is never to be the mechanical, slavish submission of subjects bowing to the orders of a tyrant. Rather, we obey out of love. The other week you highlighted the significance of the Lord's words in John: "if ye love me, [you will] keep my commandments" (14.15), "if a man love me, he will keep my words: and my Father will love him, and we will come unto him, and make our abode with him" (14.23), and "ye are my friends, if ye do whatsoever I command you" (15.14). In other words, just as real love will show itself not in lip service but in glad obedience, so true obedience springs from a heart of love for the Saviour who has done so much for us. Now this governs the whole Christian life, from corporate assembly exercises to personal day to day walk with God. "We love him because he first loved us" (1 John 4.19). Of course, our motives will never be pure. The flesh (that bubbling cauldron of evil within) so taints all we think and do that even our holiest moments are tarnished by spots of pride, complacency, self-satisfaction. But the Lord knows the heart, and sometimes our best recourse is Peter's language: "Lord, thou knowest all things; thou knowest that I love thee" (John 21.17). Do not be discouraged into inaction because you recognize that your motives are not what they ought to be (that is the way Satan hamstrings many dear saints); rather, confess your anxieties to the Lord and seek with His aid to do what is right.

Third, we have to be scrupulously precise about the **message**, as any deviation from the truth can be fatal. Paul's language is stunningly direct: "though we, or an angel from heaven, preach any other gospel unto you than that which we have preached unto you, let him be accursed. As we said before, so say I now again, If any *man* preach any other gospel unto you than that ye have received, let him be accursed" (Gal 1.8-9). Note: message takes precedence over messenger. And this is the same man who rejoiced when the right message was preached even for the wrong reasons (see Philippians 1.14-18)! You see, accuracy is essential. The greatest gospel expositor in the New Testament details the indispensable ingredients of the message in his letter to the Romans. Let's take Romans 5.1-11 as a key passage. There we are confronted with (i) *"God"* (vv.1,2,5,8,10,11), both the source and subject of that which is "the gospel of God" (Rom 1.1). In our man-centred world everything revolves around creatures who are exquisitely tender of their own dignity, but the gospel by contrast magnifies God. That is why it cannot be compromised in the slightest. Next we meet with the concept of (ii) *sin* (Paul uses a variety of terms: we are by nature "without strength", "ungodly", v.6; "sinners", v.8; "enemies", v.10), which means that man is utterly incapable of satisfying God's requirements. Because the gospel begins not with man but with God in all His majesty and holiness, the gulf between our ruin and His ineffable glory is all the more marked. We are sinners by nature (our inner disposition inherited from Adam) and practice (our deeds). This terrible condition leads us inexorably towards an even more dreadful destiny, (iii) *"wrath"* (v.9). This language describes both the outpouring of God's just anger against man's wickedness in the future Great Tribulation (Rev 6.15-17; 1 Thess 1.9-10; 5.9-10) and the eternal destiny of the lost in the lake of fire (John 3.36; Rom 9.22; Rev 20.11-15). Mercifully, such bad news is followed by the divine remedy: (iv) *"blood"* (v.9). Check these verses and you will (I hope) come to the conclusion that "blood" is biblical shorthand for a sacrificial death which satisfies all God's demands (Lev 17.11; Exod 12.13; Heb 9.22; 10.4,19; 1 Pet 1.18-19; 1 John 1.7; Rev 5.9). On the cross the Lord Jesus became His people's substitute, offering to God the payment that our sins demand. Finally, (v) "faith" (vv.1-2) is the only way into the good of the blessings listed in the first five verses. No works of men can ever please God (Rom 3.20; Titus 3.5); but simple confidence in what Christ has done unlocks the door of salvation. Now, we must be certain of this message before we can communicate it to others, and perhaps the safest way is to lock it into the text of scripture. When I was younger I marked in my Bible a chain of verses which systematically traced the way of salvation. You might find this a useful way of having key verses at your fingertips when you want to speak about the Saviour to a friend.

Alas, I have little space left to talk about **methods.** Of course, the public preaching of the word is specially commanded of God (1 Cor 1.17-21), but quiet personal witness is also exemplified in John 1 (where John Baptist, Andrew and Philip all effectively lead others to Christ), as well as in the Lord's own private interviews with sinners. John 4 is a master class in how to reach the individual. Not all are public preachers but all can say a word for the Saviour. Remember too that where God has sovereignly placed us in terms of family and work is at least part of our mission field. The believers driven out of Jerusalem by persecution took the gospel with them, so that an apparent disaster became a blessing to others (Acts 8.4). The ex-demoniac of Mark 5.18-20 had his commendable prayer to accompany the Lord unexpectedly refused, for he was instead to be the Saviour's representative in a neighbourhood which had rejected Him. This was a hard task, for family and friends are often the toughest people to reach. Then again, in the Old Testament Joseph, Daniel and the unnamed servant girl in 2 Kings 5.2-3 were faithful voices for God in adverse circumstances. But remember – our behaviour will either support or undermine our words. As someone put it, "Your life shouts so loudly I cannot hear what you say". Like the balanced bells and pomegranates on the hem of the High Priest's garment (Exod 28.33), may our life and our lips be in harmony. And may the Lord give you daily help to be a good testimony for Him.

Affectionately as always in Christ Jesus

Letter No 26:

The Pilgrim's Progress (iii)

Since this is Reading & Writing Week at university (remember the old days when you were a student?) I am less pressurized than usual and can attempt another letter. I know Bunyan never produced a *Pilgrim's Progress* Part 3 (although at least one early imitator did), but as I lie awake at night I keep thinking of new characters you might bump into in your pilgrimage to the Celestial City and they may as well (for what they are worth) see the light of day.

One rather sad fellow is **Mr Simple.** His problem is that he unthinkingly believes all he hears or reads regardless of the source. Now, we have to make a careful distinction here, because simplicity can be a spiritual positive. For example, Paul urges believers not to be corrupted from "the simplicity which is in Christ" (2 Cor 11.3), the word there meaning not naivety but sincerity or single-hearted devotion, as it does in 2 Corinthians 1.12. You can investigate with your Vine or e-Sword. That is to say, those who belong to the Saviour will not wish the brightly burning fervour of their first love to become dimmed over time. And, alas, the flame of zeal can so soon lose its brilliance, as Revelation 2.4 testifies. When we are first saved the Holy Spirit creates in us an earnest desire to be out and out for Christ, our souls longing for the daily enjoyment of His presence and the sweet sustenance of His word. The slightest disobedience brings a pang to a heart newly sensitised to sin. That is an authentic, God-honouring simplicity which we should all aim to cultivate. Cowper (in the lovely hymn, "O for a closer walk with God") mourns its all too easy loss:

> Where is the blessedness I knew
> When first I saw the Lord?
> Where is the soul-refreshing view
> Of Jesus and His word?

The whole poem is well worth reading as it contains the remedy:

> The dearest idol I have known,
> Whate'er that idol be,
> Help me to tear it from thy throne,
> And worship only thee.
>
> So shall my walk be close with God,
> Calm and serene my frame:
> So purer light shall mark the road
> That leads me to the Lamb.

May the Lord help us to walk, like Enoch (Gen 5.22; Heb 11.5), closely with Him.

In the Old Testament, by contrast, the word "simple" seems to have a very different connotation. In Proverbs 1.22 it is evidently linked with sin, while in 14.15 it describes culpable gullibility: "the simple believeth every word: but the prudent *man* looketh well to his going". Keil and Delitzsch (you have them in your e-Sword package) write about Proverbs 1.22: "Three classes of men are here addressed: the simple, who, being accessible to seduction, are only too susceptible of evil; the mockers, *i.e.*, free-thinkers; and the fools, *i.e.*, the mentally imbecile and stupid (from Arab. *kasal*, to be thick, coarse, indolent)". That is the great contrast in the Book of Proverbs: between natural folly (the consequence of sin) and God-given wisdom (Prov 1.7; 9.10). Therefore let us by all means be simple in our absolute confidence in God and His word; but when it comes to others (whether they are saved or unsaved) we have to be on our guard (1 John 4.1). Even genuine Christians can be guilty of unintentional exaggeration or misrepresentation. You will encounter some people who seem always to express themselves in fluent hyperbole and you will learn therefore to take their words with a grain of salt. Satan deceived Eve with his false logic, his specious promises, and his subtle insinuations, all aimed at stirring up a spirit of resentment against God (Gen 3.1-6). In a fallen world where even the father of lies can disguise himself as an angel of light (2 Cor 11.14; John 8.44) we have to be constantly vigilant. That is why Paul exhorts believers never to swallow what they hear without exercising careful discernment: "Prove [test, try, examine] all things; hold fast that which is good" (1 Thess 5.21). Test all you read or hear against the only infallible source of truth – God's word (Isa 8.20). The folk at Berea were commended because they checked up on the teachings of the Apostle Paul, searching their Old Testament to make sure his preaching – which presented the Lord Jesus Christ as the great fulfillment of prophecy (Rom 1.1-3) – was correct (Acts 17.11). The tragic story of the unnamed prophet in 1 Kings 13, on the other hand, is a solemn warning against incautiously accepting the claims of another. A young man who had faithfully done as the Lord commanded was led astray by an older man who lied to him (vv.15-19). And yet the young man would have been safe had he just held on to what the Lord had told him. We must not allow what others say to eclipse what we have clearly found in God's word. As someone has said, in another connection, "Never doubt in the darkness what God has taught you in the light". So don't be like poor Mr Simple, who has no quality control over what he absorbs and as a result impetuously gulps down everything, whether it is good food or poison. That is why it makes sense to get into the habit of jotting down notes when you hear the word preached, so that you can go home and check for yourself.

But not all pilgrims are negative role models. Take **Mrs Prayerful**. Every assembly has such a person – usually an elderly widow, physically frail but spiritually powerful because behind the scenes, where God alone can see, she faithfully intercedes for the saints. Paul defines a "widow indeed" as one who "trusteth in God, and continueth in supplications and prayers night and day" (1 Tim 5.5). You see, very often in a local assembly it is the elderly women who have a real grasp of the things of God, and whose diligent supplication over many years has kept the meeting going. And yet they are so frequently overlooked. In my experience widows get a raw deal in the world: cowboy builders exploit them, suppliers disregard their complaints, and local authorities fob them off. My mother used to say that if you did not have a man behind you, you counted for little. The Lord's parable of the unjust judge indicates that this is no recent phenomenon (Luke 18.1-8). But from Old Testament times the Living God has had a special concern for the downtrodden and disadvantaged, as can be seen from His instructions about the widows and fatherless in Israel (Exo 22.22-24; Psa 146.9). And the feeble can have an impact in heaven out of all proportion to their significance in the eyes of the world. The first example in the New Testament, and a good subject for a brief study, is Anna (Luke 2.36-38). When I was a student back in the 1960s/70s there was a lovely old lady in the assembly to whom I could go when I specially wanted prayer for myself or for student friends I was trying to reach for the Lord. I knew she would pray. Never undervalue those in the local assembly whose ministry seems to be low-profile. Everyone sees what a platform speaker does; but there are others in the local church whose service is just as, if not more, valuable. So often people say, "But what can *I* do for the Lord?" Well, we can *all* engage in private prayer – it's not glamorous, like preaching to big crowds, and it will not gain you any public esteem because no one but the Lord sees it. But it carries weight with God. And of all spiritual exercises it is (for me at least) the most difficult. Bible study is usually a joy, fellowship I can just about manage despite being shy, and witness ... well, I'm bad at that too – but real prayer (precisely because it is in secret) is very, very tough. Yet New Testament language is direct enough whether it is a command or a description of Paul's practice: "Praying always with all prayer and supplication in the Spirit, and watching thereunto with all perseverance and supplication for all saints" (Eph 6.18); "We give thanks to God and the Father of our Lord Jesus Christ, praying always for you" (Col 1.3). For Christian males especially there is the temptation to think that, since we are entrusted with the responsibility of taking part audibly in prayer at the gatherings of the believers (1 Tim 2.8), we can cut back on private devotion. No – we all need to continue steadfastly in what they used to call our "quiet times" of communion with the Lord. Mrs Prayerful is a standing example of faithfulness over the years. May the Lord encourage us both to be persistent in our prayer lives.

Affectionately as always in Christ Jesus

Letter No 27:

Christ's Pre-Eminence

This is just another fairly informal note to thank you once again for the refreshment of your company last night (not forgetting of course the generous lifetime's supply of peppermint tea). It was, as it always is, an encouragement to hear you pray, to see how you are steadily increasing in your grasp of spiritual things – and perhaps best of all, to note that you are becoming more and more conscious of God's mercy to you. That is a lovely thing. Never lose sight of the depths from which God in grace has plucked you, for all the glory in salvation is His. A candid recollection of what we are by nature will safeguard us against swollen heads and foolish tongues.

Good King Uzziah in the Old Testament was a fine man of God, strengthened by the Lord while he did what was right, until (alas) he became powerful and secure. Then he seems to have grown to be rather full of himself, so cocksure that he aspired to a privilege which God had *not* given him. He was Judah's king, honour enough for most men, but he wanted to be a priest as well.

> "And his name spread far abroad; for he was marvellously helped, till he was strong. But when he was strong, his heart was lifted up to *his* destruction: for he transgressed against the LORD his God, and went into the temple of the LORD to burn incense upon the altar of incense" (2 Chron 26.15-16).

Now in Old Testament times the kingly tribe in the nation of Israel was Judah (which was announced as far back as Genesis 49.10, long before Israel ever had a king), while the priestly tribe was Levi. That is why in the history of Israel you will not find a man who was both a priest *and* a king – king and prophet, yes (David, for example; Acts 2.29-31), or prophet and priest (Ezekiel 1.3), but never priest and king. You see, priests came from one tribe, kings from another, while prophets were raised up by God from any tribe. The great exception proves the rule, for Melchizedek (have you met him yet in Genesis?), who did indeed function as king and priest simultaneously, was not a member of the nation of Israel at all: "Melchizedek king of Salem brought forth bread and wine: and he *was* the priest of the most high God" (Gen 14.18). The letter to the Hebrews in the New Testament teaches us that this genuine historical contemporary of the patriarch Abraham was more that just that – he was also a foreshadowing of the Son of God. Listen:

> "For this Melchisedec, king of Salem, priest of the most high God, who met Abraham returning from the slaughter of the kings, and blessed him; To whom also Abraham gave a tenth part of all; first being by interpretation King of righteousness, and after that also King of Salem, which is, King of peace; Without father, without mother, without descent, having neither beginning of days, nor end of life; but made like unto the Son of God; abideth a priest continually" (Heb 7.1-3).

That the inspired record of Genesis fails to mention either his birth or his death (most remarkable in a book full of both!) is no accident. It is not that he entered the world in some supernatural way (for he was merely a man) but that God has so organised His word that Mechisedec stands as a little picture of the One who (as to His deity) truly had neither beginning of days nor of end of life. And as He was king of Salem *and* priest of the most high God (without being a member of the tribe of Levi, which of course did not even exist at that time, Levi not having been born) he anticipates the unique person of Christ who combines in Himself those two great offices. Hebrews teaches that the Lord Jesus Christ, born of the tribe of Judah, is a priest "after the order of [not Levi, but] Melchisedek" (Heb 7.14-17).

This is all a rather longwinded way of saying that God kept priesthood and kingship separate in Israel for a distinct reason: so as to highlight the uniqueness of His coming Messiah. He, foreshadowed in the post-exilic figure of Joshua, will truly be "a priest upon his throne" (Zechariah 6.13). Remember that in all things He must have the pre-eminence (Col 1.18). Therefore it was a very serious thing for Uzziah to try and combine what God had deliberately kept apart. Tragically, in seeking more he ended up with less. The penalty of leprosy meant that he could no longer function even as king (2 Chon 26.17-21). Lesson: let us be content with what God in His grace has given us (Jer 45.5). And after all, we have been blessed with "all spiritual blessing in the heavenlies in Christ" (Eph 1.3). God just could not have given us more. As one the speakers at our conference was saying tonight (and I am only now back from it) we are fully endowed with astonishing blessings the very instant we are saved – and it takes the rest of our Christian life to unpack and fully comprehend all those riches. When you trusted the Saviour you were instantaneously born again, justified, redeemed, reconciled, sanctified, constituted a child of God, indwelt by the Holy Spirit, gifted with a specific spiritual gift or gifts to allow you to fulfil your role in the assembly where God has placed you, made a member of the body of Christ, brought into the fellowship of God's Son, joined to a holy and a royal priesthood – and that's just eleven truths! Quick Test - can you find scriptures for them?

You are in my thoughts and prayers in relation to your family (that the Lord will have mercy on them) and your future career (that you will follow the employment of His choice). Just take each day at a time. Much of our life consists of simple obedience in mundane things – and if we walk close with God in the small things he will certainly lead us aright in the big ones.

I am really glad you are pressing on with your scripture memorisation. Psalm 2 is packed with truth. I tried to divide it up this morning into three-verse units: (i) **vv.1-3: the Hostility of the Heathen** (summing up man's ingrained hatred for God and Christ); **vv.4-6: the Laughter of the Lord** (introducing the solemnity of God's coming judgments upon man's rebellion, as outlined in Revelation chapters 6-19); (iii) **vv.7-9: the Sovereignty of the Son** (foregrounding the inevitable supremacy of Christ when He comes to reign from Jerusalem, as well as testifying to what He means to God: "Thou art my son"); (iv) **vv.10-12: Safety in Submission** (the only way to escape divine judgment is to "kiss the Son", that is to say, show humble, implicit trust in Him). How good to realise that God has opened our eyes to our danger and caused us to be eternally blessed in placing our trust in the Lord Jesus Christ. Nothing in this world can compare with the joy of knowing the Living God – for that joy lasts for ever.

Continue steadfastly in the things of God and do not let anyone discourage you. Find all your resources in the Lord Jesus and His infallible word.

Affectionately as always in Christ Jesus

WEEK TWENTY EIGHT

Letter No 28:

Praying in Public

As I wait for the men to come and install a new washing machine, I thought I'd write to you this time about public participation in prayer. I still vividly remember a painful experience from my student days when I was about 21. A godly man in the local assembly, a man for whom I had the highest esteem and who had been a tremendous spiritual help to me, happened to mention how hard he found praying in public, especially when it came to worship. His words went something like this: "I know that I am very feeble and inadequate in my expressions of praise and adoration in the assembly – and you, David, are even worse". That was the sting in the tail, and it gave me quite a start. In fact it had the long-term effect of completely silencing me in assembly gatherings for about two years. I lost all confidence and felt utterly incapable of lifting my voice to God. Words can linger long in the mind. Only very gradually did I begin again to try and take part publicly. And it is still very tough. Preaching is hard enough because one is speaking to an entire company – but prayer involves addressing the Living God of the universe on behalf of and in the presence of other believers. Those of us who are innately shy and tongue-tied find this distinctly nerve-wracking, and even natural talkers will be daunted once they grasp the enormity of the privilege. Let me therefore list, in alphabetical order, a few hints which may be of practical use to you as you fulfil your role in your local assembly (1 Tim 2.8)

First, public prayer must be **audible**. God of course knows the breathings of our hearts and reads our words before ever we utter them (Psa 139.4; Isa 65.24), but the saints, being only human, have to hear them spoken aloud. Therefore our prayers must be pitched at an adequate volume, clearly articulated and taken at a controlled pace so that all (especially the elderly) can follow us. This does not mean we have to shout, but it does require careful clarity of utterance, like the disciples who "lifted up their voice to God with one accord" (Acts 4.23). Second, prayer can be **brief**. One of the many perils of growing old (and I write as one who knows!) is that we can fall into the trap of assuming that prolixity is an infallible measure of piety. It isn't. I think the longest public prayer recorded in the Bible is Solomon's at the dedication of the temple (1 Kings 8.15-53), certainly far shorter than the 20-minute marathons some brethren produce. Mind you, we should bear in mind that some dear men have perhaps had to keep a small assembly going over many years with little support from others, and have therefore got into the habit of filling up the time. Nevertheless it makes good sense not to weary the saints with unnecessary length.

Third, prayer needs to be **considerate**. That is to, say, because we are taking part in a gathering of believers we must exercise due courtesy and "consider one another" (Heb 10.24). After all, there are other brethren who will wish to take part, so we should not hog the time, nor should we precipitately leap to our feet to get in before anyone else has the opportunity. Participation in spiritual exercises should never be unseemly, as though we were taking part in a contest. I know this is not Paul's meaning when he says "tarry one for another" (1 Cor 11.33), but his words do sum up what our attitude should be. As a young fellow, I have sat through prayer meetings where older men have covered everything under the sun and left me wracking my brains for something left to pray about. So do not aim to be exhaustive. The best thing is to come along to the prayer meeting with one or two specific matters on your heart which you can lay before the Lord, just as at the Lord's Supper we tend to have a few prepared thoughts which we can use in our worship. Fourth, prayer should be appropriately **dignified**. Since we are addressing the God of heaven we should, like Abraham, approach Him with reverence (Gen 18.27). Some people think reverence is attained through the cultivation of an unnatural incantatory "prayer voice", far removed from normal speech. This is absurd and just sounds artificial. Rather, aim for a fitting register of language which indicates respect. The idiom of the AV provides a good model which has helped generations of believers. Those of us raised under the sound of its cadences often find that its archaic pronouns and inflections actually aid our prayers in constantly reminding us that we are speaking to One who is gloriously different from all others. But whether we employ the rich formality of the AV or not (and this is a matter where it would be unwise to dictate) we should always keep uppermost in our minds that we are addressing the God of infinite majesty. Casualness, triteness, over-familiarity should be avoided. As Solomon advises, "Be not rash with thy mouth, and let not thine heart be hasty to utter *any* thing before God: for God *is* in heaven, and thou upon earth: therefore let thy words be few" (Eccles 5.2).

Fifth, our prayers should be **easy** in the sense of "easy to be understood" (1 Cor 14.9). Although the word "eloquent" sprang to mind for the letter E, I have deliberately rejected a term that tends to imply a skilful, possibly glib fluency of tongue, which is not what prayer is about at all. Often our words will be stumbling and inept because we find it hard to express our deepest feelings before God. But that matters little as the Lord knows our hearts. What *is* important is that our brethren and sisters are able to follow what we are saying, because the scripture assumes that they will wish to record their agreement with our words by adding "Amen [so be it]" at the close of our prayer (1 Chron 16.36; 1 Cor 14.16). Never forget that you are not alone when you pray publicly – the saints wish to hear, understand and enjoy what you are saying. Sixth, prayer is **functional** in that it will be conditioned by the special character of the meeting in which we take part. Remember the purpose of each gathering. At the Lord's Supper we aim to remember the Lord Jesus, so our prayers will focus on Him and not on our needs or the work of the assembly. If you have a prayer meeting just before the gospel meeting it is primarily to implore God's help in the following evangelistic gathering. The weekly assembly prayer meeting is, on the other hand, an occasion when every aspect of prayer (supplication, intercession, thanksgiving and worship) is entirely appropriate (1 Tim 2.1).

Seventh, because of its **group** context (for we pray representatively on behalf of the whole company), what may be suitable for the private sphere is often out of place in the public. In the prayer meeting we pray 'we/us' (singular pronouns can sound awkwardly intrusive) while in private it will be 'I/me'.

Eighth, prayer should be **helpful**, a positive encouragement to God's people. If you have specific matters for which you wish to request prayer (and that is exactly what the prayer meeting is for, as Acts 4.23-31 indicates), it is better to announce this information clearly to the whole assembly beforehand, rather than embark upon a cryptic prayer which leaves folk confused.

Ninth, prayer ought to be **intelligent** and make sense. Our approach to God will best conform to the basic pattern in the Bible, which teaches that "through him [Christ] we both [saved Jews and Gentiles] have access by one Spirit unto the Father" (Eph 2.18). That is, we speak *to* the Father *in the name of* the Son (John 16.23) *in the energy of* the Holy Spirit (Jude 20). Keep this in mind and you will never muddle the persons of the Godhead. I find it useful to direct my prayers to "our God and Father", or some similar phrase (1 Pet 1.3), rather than to the "Lord", as it is all too easy with the latter title to forget whether one is speaking to the Father or the Son. It would, for example, be plainly wrong to thank the Father for dying for us, or praise the Son for sending the Father. Of course, the best resource for prayer is the scriptures as a whole. The better we know the Book the better we shall speak to our God. May the Lord help us both to discharge our public responsibility as we ought, for His glory.

Affectionately as always in Christ Jesus

Letter No 29:

The Pilgrim's Progress (iv)

Time for yet another instalment of *The Pilgrim's Progress*! I have two new characters to introduce, characters who have come to mind largely because I have been exposed to both of them over recent days.

The first is **Mr Grunter**. You may not have met him yet, but doubtless you will. This is the brother who, while another is praying in an assembly meeting, audibly expresses his approbation by means of a continual series of loud assents, such as "Amen, yes Lord! Hallelujah! Mmm, aaarrrr", and so on. Some of Mr Grunter's ejaculations are beyond ordinary spelling. Now of course it is a very good thing that we pay intelligent attention to what our brethren say in prayer to the Lord. After all, they represent the thoughts of the whole company. Sadly, I have known men to flick through their hymnbooks or engage in Bible reading while others are leading in prayer – conduct which would be discourteous in a secular context and is bordering on the irreverent when we are gathered in the presence of God. Further, it is both biblical and fitting that we register our agreement with what has been uttered before the Lord by saying "Amen" at the close of the prayer (1 Chron 16.36; Rev 5.14). And to do him justice, it may be that Mr Grunter sincerely imagines that his mutterings are a real support to the brethren who pray. He is, in my experience at least, usually a man of dominating personality who assumes that everyone is like himself.

But to engage in a vocal running commentary while another is seeking to speak publicly to the God of heaven is entirely inappropriate. First of all it is distracting, both for the brother engaged in prayer and for the company who are listening. What may be intended to be an encouragement is in practice more often a disturbance. Mr Grunter is not noted for speaking in a discreet *sotto voce*. Public prayer at the best of times is a demanding exercise, involving coherence of thought and solemnity of soul.

Unnecessary and intrusive background noises are not liable to help spiritual concentration. Second, it is disorderly. At the close of his long chapter on the principles governing vocal participation in church gatherings, Paul writes "Let all things be done decently and in order" (1 Cor 14.40). The first key word ("decently") means "in a seemly manner"; the second ("order") indicates arrangement, or orderly condition. Certainly a prima facie reading of this verse would slap a ban upon any behaviour likely to compromise that holy decorum which suits an assembly of saints. There is an overt self-indulgence about such noisy interference in the gathering which suggests a distinct lack of self-control. Third, it is irreverent because it serves only to draw attention to Mr Grunter, which is not the purpose of any gathering to the name of the Lord Jesus. When believers meet to break bread they do this to honour the person and work of Christ. All we do there is designed to uplift Him. But Mr Grunter's actions simply foreground his own presence. When I was a student a contemporary in the local assembly used to come along to the breaking of bread meeting wearing a purple cape. Now even in those remote days a cape (let alone a purple one) was not your common or garden student attire. So he stood out. He was not, as I recall, a particularly vocal fellow, his flamboyance being restricted to his dress. Nevertheless he was truly Mr Grunter's nephew in that his presence was anything but self-effacing. Insistent attention-seeking suggests a serious misunderstanding of the Christian's role in service and worship.

Let us therefore pay respectful attention to the public prayers of our brethren; let us weigh their words and add our amen when they have concluded what they have to say. But let us not so far forget ourselves as to think we are of such spiritual significance that the saints must be constantly reminded we are there. The three disciples on the mountain who "saw no man save Jesus only" (Matt 17.8) were taken up, not with one another, not even with the two great Old Testament figures who had briefly joined that select company, but with Christ. That should be our aim when we meet to remember the Saviour. Indeed, our actions in all gatherings of believers should aim to exalt Him while keeping ourselves in the shade.

In striking contrast to Mr Grunter is **Mr Expositor**. Frequently a quiet, unassuming man in private life, he speaks with great authority and clarity from the platform. I knew such a man when I was a student, and I have had the privilege of encountering others since, although they are by no means thick on the ground. This man follows in the footsteps of Ezra the scribe and his colleagues who, in the days after Israel's return from Babylonian exile, sought to open up the scriptures for God's people to understand:

> "And Ezra the scribe stood upon a pulpit of wood, which they had made for the purpose. . .And Ezra opened the book in the sight of all the people; (for he was above all the people;) and when he opened it, all the people stood up:. . .[and, along with the Levites, he] caused the people to understand the law: and the people *stood* in their place. . .So they read in the book in the law of God distinctly, and gave the sense, and caused *them* to understand the reading" (Nehemiah 8.4-8).

That is a recipe for really helping the saints. Of course, in order to make scripture clear to others it must be clear to us – so there will be much behind-the-scenes study before ever Mr Expositor can effectively teach the word. The few minutes he spends on the platform are but the tip of the iceberg of preparation. Further, he exalts scripture rather than himself. Therefore he will make sure that something as seemingly simple as the public reading of God's word is done well. He will read enough for his select passage to make sense, he will read accurately since he believes in verbal inspiration, he will read with intelligent emphasis so that the passage is illuminated, he will read compellingly because he loves the word, he will read without that unbecoming haste which so often gives the impression that a speaker is more interested in what he has to say about the scriptures than in the pure word itself. After all, Mr Expositor knows that his own comments may be erroneous – whereas the word of truth can never be. It is a great thing just to read the word aloud. But it demands practice. And only those who have attempted to do it themselves know how much time Mr Expositor spends alone with his Bible.

If he follows Ezra in his presentation, he emulates Paul in his curriculum, being concerned to teach "the whole counsel of God" (Acts 20.27) without fear or favour. Some of us love particular parts of the word, especially those which are comforting rather than demanding, but Mr Expositor will faithfully teach it all. You will therefore normally hear him opening up an entire chapter or paragraph of the Bible in detail, often going through it verse by verse to make sure his auditors are in no doubt as to its meaning. That is the way to teach the word. It is hard, it is (much of the time) lonely, it is demanding. But it is worth it.

The lessons are clear enough. May the Lord graciously help us to be a positive, practical benefit to His people by occupying their thoughts with Christ and the word.

Affectionately as always in Christ Jesus

Letter No 30:

A Lifting Up for the Downcast

One of the rather odd benefits of having a bad week is that it casts us on the Lord. As the Arab proverb says, it's all sunshine that makes a desert. Certainly the common experience of believers is that when things seem to be going smoothly we become less vigilant, less spiritually alert, less concerned to please the Lord. Prosperity blunts our spiritual edge. And that is precisely when God, in His grace, steps in to shake us up. Come the storm and we hasten swiftly home. A recent Choice Gleanings quoted the words of Thomas Watson: "When God lays men upon their backs then they look up to heaven". Well, the last few days have been particularly frustrating and difficult for me, so I thought I would write you another of my little letters, this one entitled *A Lifting Up for the Downcast*. Since God's educational programme for His children involves valleys as well as mountain tops (and considerably more of the former than the latter), you may find it helpful to store up this information for the future. I cannot claim originality for the caption, as a puritan called William Bridge preached a series of messages from Psalm 42.11 under that title in 1648. Nevertheless, seeing an old paperback edition while emptying out a bookcase in order to make room in my hallway for men to move in a new washing machine, I was reminded of the encouragement such a title can provide.

For any believer going through times of trial and crisis let me suggest that consolation is found in resting on three great pillows of comfort in the word. The first is the doctrine of **eternal security**. This is that gracious assurance that each one who belongs to the Lord Jesus Christ is safe for ever. It is, of course, part and parcel of God's "so great salvation" (Heb 2.3). One of the fundamental differences between biblical salvation and man-made religion is that anything man produces is entirely dependent upon man and therefore permanently vulnerable. Good works, rituals, morality, they are all a broken reed. But what God does is perfect and eternal (Eccles 3.14). And since salvation is of the Lord it lasts. A classic passage is John 10, where the Lord Jesus says that His sheep "shall never perish" (v.28). Of course, we must be clear about the identity of the sheep before we can appropriate their security. Who are the Lord's sheep? Certainly not the entire population of Israel, for "he came unto his own, and his own [the nation of Israel viewed as a whole] received him not" (John 1.11). But some did. The characteristic of Christ's sheep is that they hear His voice (John 10.3,16,27), a metaphor for saving faith in His person and work. Therefore the Lord's sheep in John 10 are first of all the elect remnant of Israel (10.2-5). And there are more. "Other sheep I have which are not of this fold; them also I must bring" (John 10.16). Outside the fold of Judaism with all its God-given laws and ordinances are Gentiles like you and me, yet the Lord Jesus has a chosen people there as well, a people who will be brought to Him through the preaching of the gospel. His sheep then are elect Jews and Gentiles who, led to faith in Him, constitute the "one flock" of which He is the centre and shepherd (v.16). But to the hostile Jewish religious leaders He says, "ye believe not, because ye are not of my sheep" (10.26). This startling verse needs to be read carefully. It is not unbelief which prevents them from being His sheep; rather, because they are not His sheep they do not believe. The same truth is taught in John 8.47 and Acts 13.48. The Lord's people are His even before they hear and respond to the gospel. All this anticipates Ephesians 1.3, which tells believers that they were chosen in Christ "before the foundation of the world". As the old lady said to Spurgeon, "I am so glad the Lord chose me before I was born, because He would never have done so afterwards!" Quite so. McCheyne's hymn reminds me that I was "chosen not for good in me". Yes, salvation is completely of the Lord.

So wherein lies our security? Look at the marvellous promises of verses 27-30. First, there are two GIFTS. We are unworthy recipients of the Lord's free gift of eternal life, but we were ourselves given by the Father to the Son in eternity past (John 17.2,6). Second, there are two GRASPS. Christ's sheep are held fast in His own hand and in the Father's hand simultaneously. We just cannot be safer. Third, there are two GUARANTORS. Father and Son, though distinct, are "one" in purpose and activity, for there can be no disagreement between the persons of the Godhead. And they pledge our everlasting safekeeping. When you feel low, just pause to remember what God has done eternally and irreversibly for your soul.

The second pillow is **divine sovereignty**. When I was younger I found this truth so disturbing that I endeavoured to avoid it. Now, by contrast, it is to me one of the sweetest doctrines in the word of God. Basically it means that God is in absolute control of His universe, and cannot be thwarted in the fulfilment of His programme. Listen to Psalm 115.2-3:

> "Wherefore should the heathen say, Where *is* now their God?
> But our God *is* in the heavens: he hath done whatsoever he
> hath pleased".

Our God is no absentee landlord like the false god of the 18th century deists who, as you will remember, proposed that some First Cause had created the universe but then abandoned it to its own devices. No, the God of creation is also the God of providence (Col 1.16-17; Heb 1.1-3). He actively superintends the actions, the circumstances, the destinies of His people. Now, this does not mean that human beings are freed from personal responsibility; on the contrary, men are accountable to God for what they do. For its careful preservation of balancing truths Peter's masterly summary cannot be bettered: "Him [the Lord Jesus], being delivered by the determinate counsel and foreknowledge of God [divine sovereignty] ye have taken, and by wicked hands have crucified and slain [human responsibility]" (Acts 2.23). God always maintains supreme control. Years ago, I was stuck in a delayed train somewhere between Carlisle and a destination in England where I was supposed to be taking a Bible teaching weekend. And I was becoming more and more uneasy because I knew I would not reach the meeting in time. It was then that Ephesians 1.11 forcibly struck me as never before. Our God is the One "who worketh all things after the counsel of his own will". What a glorious description of God! Do not miss the delightfully comprehensive "all things", worth comparing with its twin in Romans 8.28. That relieved the stress: although I might be late for the meeting God had a purpose in it all. Further, the very delay was beneficial in teaching me a valuable theological lesson. Our God knows what He's doing with us, and His ultimate purpose is to make us like His Son (Rom 8.28-30). When things seem to go wrong, we have to learn to rest our heads on the soft pillow of divine sovereignty.

Third is the doctrine of **instant accessibility**. To know our salvation is secure and that the God who loves us has a constant care for each of His people is a soothing medicine in time of trouble. But there is more. God is instantly accessible every day of the week, every hour of the day, every minute of the hour (Psa 50.15; Heb 4.14-16). Financial assets may be so tied up by the bank that they are untouchable, but the Lord is ever at hand for His people (Heb 13.5-6).   Whenever we need Him He is contactable in prayer. I have no space to develop this further but I hope you follow my argument: weary heads can find perfect rest on these pillows of support. The downcast can be lifted up by meditating on the sweetness of God's irrevocable promises. Stock your heart with them now, in days of plenty, so that when famine comes you will be ready.

Affectionately as always in Christ Jesus

Letter No 31:

Christ in Hebrews

Since you have graduated from the Pentateuch to Hebrews, the great New Testament exposition of the Old Testament, I thought I'd try and encourage you a little by suggesting ways in which it presents the Lord Jesus. As I said the other day, it took me many years to get to grips with its teaching, for it is by no means an easy read. Angels and high priests and tabernacles do not seem particularly relevant to the believer's daily life. Nor does it address practical matters of conduct like James, or local assembly principles like 1 Corinthians, or even the doctrinal significance of the gospel message like Romans. One cannot really make sense of it until one has read about the Old Testament sacrificial system, priesthood, covenants, and the like. But what does come over right from the start is that the central person in the letter – and indeed in the entire universe – is the Lord Jesus Christ. And to recognise His pre-eminence in everything is one of the most practical things in the world, for once He is in His rightful place all else falls into place. So here (much condensed!) is Christ in Hebrews.

To demonstrate the greatness of Christ Jesus, the writer's strategy is to compare and contrast Him with major figures of biblical history, celebrities in whom the Jews so gladly rejoiced. Christ is better than them all. First, He is **more excellent than the prophets** (1.1-2). A prophet was God's mouthpiece, possessing authority by virtue of his service (Amos 3.7). Yet all the prophets together were only preliminary ("in time past"), looking forward to One yet to come; they were piecemeal in their revelation ("sundry times and divers manners"), providing a bit by bit disclosure of the divine message over many years and by various means; and they were plural ("prophets"), a host of mainly unnamed servants. By contrast the Lord Jesus is the final prophet, for there is nothing beyond God's revelation in Him. And He is the comprehensive prophet, for God has spoken fully "in Son" (as though He was God's language). In Christ there is one great unified expression of all God's mind. He uniquely fulfils the Old Testament expectations of a prophet like Moses (Deut 18.15-18; John 8.25-28). In short, God has nothing more to say (John 1.1,14).

Second, He is **more excellent than angels** (1.4-7). Although the Bible teaches the power of angels (2 Kings 19.35; Matt 28. 2-4; 2 Pet 2.11), they are but creatures ("maketh", v.7), while Christ is Creator (1.10; John 1.1-3; Col 1.15-17). They are servants ("ministers", vv.7,14; Mark 1.13), whereas the Lord Jesus is the Son (v.5); and they are worshippers (v.6), while Christ is the grand object of worship (v.6; Rev 5.6-8,11-13).

Third, He is **more excellent than Adam** (2.6-9). Unfallen Adam and Eve (Gen 1.26-28) were upright, intelligent, innocent, in fellowship with God, and entrusted with responsibility for the created world. The Hebrew writer summarises man's dignity (v.7a; not a little higher than the monkeys, but a little lower than the angels), dominion (vv.7,8, giving the lie to the presuppositions of animal rights movements), and tragic disobedience (v.8b, expressed in the obvious ruin of man's place on the planet). So we turn thankfully from "man" (v.6) to "Jesus" (v.9), the special name of the Son's humiliation. Notice His amazing stoop (v.9), becoming "a little lower than angels" that He might suffer (v.9), for He who had all dominion voluntarily took the place of the lowest at Calvary so that He might for ever deal with the problem of sin. But there follows His exaltation (v.9) for, in virtue of all He endured, He is now "crowned with glory and honour". God has magnificently compensated Him for the Cross. And there will be yet more to come when He reigns over this planet in the millennium, fulfilling the mandate of Psalm 8. Adam, though great in privilege, was a failure, but the Lord Jesus Christ is the perfect fulfilment of all God's purpose for man.

Fourth, He is **more excellent than Moses** (3.1-6). Numbers 12.1-8 (the passage used in Hebrews) illustrates Moses's significance both officially and personally. He was faithful (vv.2,5) in his loyalty to God's commands: when all Israel, including his own family, defected, he stood firm. He was "worthy of glory" (v.3), experiencing a remarkable transfiguration when the reflection of divine brightness lingered in his face (Exod 34.29-30; 2 Cor 3.7). He was a servant in God's house (v.5). But the Lord Jesus far exceeds this, being marked by impeccable faithfulness (v.2). He is "worthy of *more* glory" (v.3), shown on the mount where He radiated rather than merely reflected divine glory (Matt 17.1,2,8). He is "Son over the house" (v.6) for, despite His service, He remains eternally the unique Son. Moses, God's messenger and apostle to Israel, has been completely superseded by Christ (John 1.17).

Fifth, He is **more excellent than Joshua** (4.8-9; see Newberry margin). While Joshua bore witness in name to the truth that "Jehovah is Saviour", Christ was this in His very nature as God manifest in the flesh (Matt 1.21). Joshua's people ("them" refers to Israel, v.8) were the nation he led into the promised land, but the Lord Jesus deals with "the people of God" (v.9), an innumerable company including believing Jews and Gentiles. And while Joshua gave Israel a material land, this was merely a faint picture of the eternal rest of soul available to all who, turning from their own works, by faith cling solely to the work of Christ for their salvation (v.10).

Sixth, He is **more excellent than Aaron** (4.14 - 5.10) Israel's high priest: as the nation's representative, he alone entered God's presence on their behalf. We note his humanity ("taken from among men", 5.1a), ministry ("to offer gifts and sacrifices", 5.1b), and sympathy ("compassed with infirmity", 5.2,3). But the Lord Jesus is far greater. His humanity, as real as Aaron's, is joined to eternal deity ("Jesus the son of God", 4.14), His ministry infinitely more effective ("author of eternal salvation", 5.9), and His sympathy more reliable (for He was "in all points tempted like as we are, sin apart", 4.15). Unlike Aaron, Christ endured all that Satan could throw at Him, and remains unchangeably sinless in the intrinsic holiness of His Being. In our great high priest we find both unfailing sympathy and unshakeable strength.

Seventh, He is **more excellent than Melchisedek** (7.1-3), that mysterious person who appears only in Genesis 14 and Psalm 110. That he was "made like unto" the Son of God (7.3) indicates that Christ, not Melchisedek, is the ultimate measure of splendour. Melchisedek was king (7.1) of a city called Salem ("peace"), but Christ is king of kings (Rev 1.5; 19.16), giving real and lasting peace to all who belong to Him (Eph 2.14). Melchisedek was priest of the most high God (7.1), but our Saviour is "great high priest" (4.14). And while Melchisedek blessed one man, providing refreshment after a battle (7.1), Christ's people (7.25) are blessed with all spiritual blessings in the heavenlies (Eph 1.3).

Eighth, He is **more excellent than all the sacrifices** (10.1-10). The entire Old Testament sacrificial system pointed to Him. In themselves, the offerings did nothing for man or God, for they were only tokens of Calvary.

Hebrews argues that they were unavailing (10.1,4), unable to deal with sins; unceasing (10.2,3) in their repetition, thus demonstrating their inadequacy; and unpleasing (10.8), because they could not satisfy God. The answer to failing offerings is the person of Christ Jesus: "Lo, I come" (10.7). The Son came from heaven to provide a sacrifice that was effectual and eternal (10.12,14).

Finally, He is **more excellent than all the heroes of faith** (11). Hebrews 11 lists people who exemplified practical confidence in God and His word (Rom 10.17). But they pale into insignificance compared with "Jesus", for they were but examples, while He is the leader of faith (12.2), manifesting it perfectly in His life. As a great cloud of witnesses they provide encouragement, but He alone is the object of our gaze (12.2,3). They endured persecution but He uniquely endured the cross (12.2).

In short, throughout Hebrews the writer argues that the many give place to the One, failures are set aside in the presence of perfection, pictures are eclipsed by the reality, and the dying are superseded by the Living One - the Lord Jesus Christ. To read this book will enlarge our appreciation of the Saviour who "obtained eternal redemption for us" (9.12).

Affectionately as always in Christ Jesus

WEEK THIRTY TWO

Letter No 32:

The Prophetic Accuracy of the Bible

Lying in bed last night I began thinking about the evidences we have for the inspiration of the Bible. Its life-transforming power is one (there is no book like this); its internal consistency is another. Then there is its candid exposure of the human heart (my heart and yours) in all its folly and depravity – hardly likely to be the work of mere men. But perhaps the most outstanding testimony to biblical authority is its prophetic accuracy. Back in Old Testament times God challenged the idols of the heathen to a contest, inviting them to bring forth proofs of their reality and power. Just as in earlier days Elijah exposed the emptiness of Baalism (1 Kings 18.21-24) so Jehovah throws down the gauntlet to everything that claims deity:

> "Produce your cause, saith the LORD; bring forth your strong *reasons*, saith the King of Jacob. Let them bring *them* forth, and shew us what shall happen: let them shew the former things, what they *be*, that we may consider them, and know the latter end of them; or declare us things for to come. Shew the things that are to come hereafter, that we may know that ye *are* gods: yea, do good, or do evil, that we may be dismayed, and behold *it* together. Behold, ye *are* of nothing, and your work of nought: an abomination *is he that* chooseth you" (Isa 41.21-4).

Revealing things to come is exactly what the God of the Bible, the One who knows the end from the beginning, can do infallibly (Isa 46.9-10). Predictions written hundreds of years before the Lord Jesus was born were fulfilled to the letter in His life and ministry. And it is impossible to dismiss these as coincidences (there are far too many for a start) or argue that He was wilfully manipulating messianic expectation. Take for example John chapter 19 where we find four specific instances of Old Testament quotation. First, in verses 23-24 we have what we might call **unconscious fulfilment of prophetic poetry**. Those Roman soldiers who divided the Saviour's clothes and then gambled for His seamless coat were by no stretch of the imagination deliberately acting out the minutiae of a one thousand year old poem. After all, they knew nothing of the Hebrew scriptures; the property of executed criminals was their normal perquisite even if in this case there was one unusual item they thought too valuable to rip into pieces. And yet this group of hardened men were fulfilling the words of Psalm 22.18 which mentioned in advance both the dividing of His clothes and the gambling. Human ignorance cannot frustrate the implementation of the prophetic word.

Second, in verses 28-29 the **Lord Himself deliberately initiates the fulfilment** of two passages: Psalm 22.15 (which describes Messiah's thirst) and Psalm 69.21b (which predicts the callous offer of vinegar). These verses teach both the genuine humanity of Christ (for He who created all the water that fills the earth submitted to the experience of thirst) and the ingrained hostility of men against God's Son. In His life the Saviour always honoured the word, and as death approach He reaffirmed its total prophetic reliability (Luke 22.37; Matt 26.53-54). Thus the Living Word (John 1.1) guarantees the accomplishment of the written word.

But then we have disclosed in John 19.31-36 the **real meaning of a Jewish ceremony**. John's quotation is interesting. Having described the soldiers' action in breaking the legs of the other crucified men (to hasten death, thus satisfying the demand of the Jewish leaders who wanted all the distasteful business of crucifixion out of the way before the Sabbath) he goes on: "For these things were done, that the scripture should be fulfilled, A bone of him shall not be broken" (v.36). But which scripture? There are three possible passages. Exodus 12.46 gives the original Passover instruction that no bone of the lamb slain, roasted and eaten was to be broken. Numbers 9.27 (which uses similar language) relates to the special provision for Israelites in the wilderness who, by reason of some uncleanness, were unable to partake of the Passover on the set date. Psalm 34.19-20 refers to the sufferings of the righteous man in an ungodly world, assuring him of divine deliverance: "He keepeth all his bones: not one of them is broken". Of course, the Lord Jesus Christ is the answer to the Passover lamb (1 Cor 5.7), and He is also the perfectly righteous man (1 John 2.1). John's gospel begins with a Passover announcement: "Behold the lamb of God" (1.29). And like that lamb, Christ was selected by God (Exod 12.3), spotless (1 Pet 1.18-19), scrutinized by men (Luke 6.7), submissive before His enemies (Mark 15.4-5), and finally slain. It seems almost as if Satan, in a desperate effort to fracture a scripture (which John 10.35 tells us cannot be done), incited the authorities to order the smashing of the men's legs so that they would quickly suffocate. But the Roman soldiers, having performed this barbaric act on the robbers alongside the Saviour, came and found Him dead already. That in itself is a wonderful evidence of the uniqueness of His death, for He died when He willed to die. Remember John 10.18 ("No man taketh [my life] from me, but I lay it down of myself. I have power to lay it down, and I have power to take it again"). The language of John 19.30 is clear: "When therefore Jesus had received the vinegar, he said, It is finished; and having bowed his head, he delivered up his spirit" (Darby's translation). Notice: the Lord deliberately bowed His head and then delivered up His spirit, which is exactly the opposite of what we might expect. A victim of crucifixion dies, losing control over his body so that his head slumps onto his chest. But Christ died the other way round. He consciously rested His head and then dismissed His spirit. There was thus no need to break His legs. The tiniest detail of the Passover ritual found its fulfilment in Christ's death. Not even satanic malice can thwart God's word.

But there is more. John 19.37 records a fascinating example of the **partial fulfilment of prophecy**. Immediately after death the Saviour's body was exposed to instant and apparently arbitrary human brutality. In a pointless gesture of spite and mindless violence a Roman soldier pierced His side. But there is nothing accidental in God's universe. Even that action confirmed the word, for "another scripture saith, They shall look on him whom they pierced" (John 19.37). Now here we must carefully note John's linguistic precision. In verses 24, 28 and 36 the narrative specifies fulfilment ("that the scripture should be fulfilled"); here it is simply "another scripture saith". Why does John vary his formula? Not, I think, for the sake of literary variety but because the prophecy to which he refers (Zech 12.10) was not exhausted at Calvary. There are, you see, two distinct parts to this remarkable prediction: the piercing (which happened when the Lord died, according to John 19.34) and the looking (which will not take place until the Saviour returns in glory to be recognized by a repentant Israel, as noted in Revelation 1.7). A Roman spear may have done the piercing, but the nation was held responsible for rejecting its Messiah; and when He appears in glory "they shall look on me whom they have pierced" (Zech 12.10). Zechariah's language markedly identifies the pierced one with Jehovah Himself. It is therefore worth bearing in mind that biblical prophecy can be divided into two kinds: that which was fulfilled at the first coming of Christ, and that which will be fulfilled at His second coming.

This Peter does in Acts 3, meticulously distinguishing between (i) advance announcements of His sufferings in verse 18 ("those things, which God before had shewed by the mouth of all his prophets, that Christ should suffer, he hath so fulfilled") and (ii) predictions of His still future glory in verses 19-24 ("times of refreshing shall come from the presence of the Lord; And he shall send Jesus Christ, which before was preached unto you: Whom the heaven must receive until the times of restitution of all things, which God hath spoken by the mouth of all his holy prophets since the world began"). The scrupulously accurate accomplishment of the first guarantees the equally reliable fulfilment of the latter. No wonder the psalmist could exclaim, "For ever, O LORD, thy word is settled in heaven" (Psa 119.89). God's word is sure! Let that encourage you to trust Him and endeavor to live for Him all the more. Keep on going.

Affectionately as always in Christ Jesus

A Christmas Letter

You asked for a letter about Christmas – so here it is! I recall a friend years ago telling me he had been asked to give a talk on the topic "What the Bible says about Christmas". He smiled: "It's going to be a very short talk!" It's a bit like the old tract entitled "What the Bible teaches about Infant Baptism". You open it up only to find blank pages. You see, the traditions of Christendom always have to be tested against God's word, for many of them, though hoary with age, have no basis in scripture at all. Without doubt the Bible records the historical event of the nativity (the birth of the Lord Jesus Christ) and explains that this was no ordinary birth but rather an incarnation, the entrance into this world in real, sinless manhood of God the Son. But nowhere are believers required to commemorate this with an annual festival. Indeed, annual feasts were distinctive features of Israel, God's Old Testament people, celebrating their past and anticipating their future. Thus, for example, the Passover both looked back to the nation's historic rescue from Egyptian slavery (Exod 12) and forward to the redemptive death of Christ as the Lamb of God (John 1.29; 1 Cor 5.7). But Christians have been liberated from bondage to Jewish rituals. That is why Paul can say, "Let no man therefore judge you in meat, or in drink, or in respect of an holyday, or of the new moon, or of the sabbath *days*: Which are a shadow of things to come; but the body *is* of Christ" (Col 2.16-17). As Gentiles we were never under Jewish ceremonial law at all, but in any case salvation frees us from observances which were at best only temporary foretastes of what we now enjoy fully in Christ (Gal 5.1). So Christmas, with all its traditional religious associations, is far removed from the purity of New Testament Christianity. What the Lord Jesus left His people was not a calendar of ostentatious yearly observances, surrounded by all the showy pomp and ceremony of ecclesiastical dignity, but a simple weekly remembrance.

What therefore really happened two thousand years ago at Bethlehem? Let me offer four answers. First, there took place the **incarnation of the Son of God** (which, drained of the Latinism, means enfleshment). This is that amazing miracle whereby the Son of God, voluntarily and in fulfilment of the divine purpose, added to His eternally immutable deity sinless spotless humanity. Notice the clear language of John 1.14: "And the Word was made flesh, and dwelt among us". This was no passing phase, no mere temporary simulation of human shape such as might be undertaken by an angel (as for example in Genesis 19.1-5), but rather a genuine, eternal incorporation of manhood into the Godhead. No wonder Paul says "without controversy great is the mystery of godliness: God was manifest in the flesh" (1 Tim 3.16). Yes, the Son took a body of real flesh and blood so that, among other things, He might be able to die for His people. The Hebrew writer particularly underlines the genuineness of that body: "forasmuch then as the children are partakers of flesh and blood, he also himself likewise took part of the same" (Heb 2.14). The emphatic series of apparent synonyms drives home the point: "he also himself likewise". And His humanity was, one might say, more representative even that that of the first man Adam, for Adam was uniquely created as a mature man whereas the Saviour entered humanity through natural birth. His conception, of course, was gloriously supernatural ("behold, a virgin shall conceive and bear a son", Isa 7.14) but the birth itself was normal. Now the incarnation involved a deliberate self-humbling. John tells us that He "dwelt among us"; but his verb means to tabernacle, to pitch a tent. That is, although the Lord's humanity was wonderfully permanent (for He has taken it into heaven and will return as a visible glorious man in accordance with Revelation 1.7 and Philippians 3.20-21) His lowly sojourn among men at His first advent was only temporary. Like Israel's Old Testament travelling sanctuary the Lord Jesus, during the thirty-three or so years of His earthly visit, was outwardly unspectacular (Isa 53.2). And yet His incarnation by no means diluted His deity. To paraphrase someone else's words, although He became what He had never been before (man), He never ceased to be what He always was (God), for "in him dwelleth [this time a different word, meaning 'to house permanently'] all the fullness of the Godhead bodily" (Col 2.9). Our Saviour is none other than the perfect man and the Living God.

Second, because of the miracle at Bethlehem we have a clear **revelation of the Father**, for it is only through the Son that the Father is properly known. John 1.18 indicates that even in the Old Testament it was the Son who communicated with men. That is to say, every display of divine glory (God walking in the garden in Genesis 3, communing with Abraham in

Genesis 18, disclosing Himself to Moses in Exodus 34.5-6) was in fact a display of the Son. To put it theologically (which may not help!), all Old Testament theophanies are Christophanies. For example, in John 12.39-42 we learn specifically that the glorious being seen in Isaiah 6 ("the Lord sitting upon a throne, high and lifted up") was none other than the one we know as the Lord Jesus Christ. Bearing this in mind, we can perhaps understand why, when Philip asked if the disciples might be allowed to see the Father, the Lord replied with gentle asperity: "Have I been so long time with you, and yet hast thou not known me, Philip? He that hath seen me hath seen the Father" (John 14.9). In other words, there is no greater experience awaiting us beyond knowing the Lord Jesus – in having Him we have all.

Third, the event at Bethlehem provides a **validation of the word**, because He who is the eternal Word (John 1.1) from birth onwards always honoured the written word. The New Testament starts by looking back to the expectations of the Old and presents the Lord Jesus as the ultimate fulfilment of God's promises to David (2 Sam 7.12-16) and Abraham (Gen 22.15-18): "The book of the generation of Jesus Christ, the son of David, the son of Abraham". David's son would be Israel's coming king, while Abraham's would bring blessing to the entire planet. Now of course David had a son called Solomon, under whose reign Israel enjoyed the grandest period of prosperity and peace in their national history (1 Kings 4.24-25) – but still he falls far short of the ultimate fulfilment yet to be seen in Christ. Further, Abraham's beloved son was Isaac, one he was told to offer up to God on Mount Moriah (Gen 22.1-2) – yet that sacrifice was halted, whereas the Father truly offered up His only begotten Son for us at Calvary (Romans 8.32). Matthew sets the tone for the gospel records as a whole with his insistent reiteration of formulae like "that it might be fulfilled" (Matt 1.21-22). Predictions about the seed of the woman (Gen 3.15), Immanuel (Isa 7.14), the prince of peace (Isa 9.6-7) were, in part at least, fulfilled in the Saviour's birth. Yes, the nativity event proves the reliability of God's word.

Fourth, Bethlehem illustrates the operations of God's providence, the divine **organisation of history**. Why should Joseph and Mary, who lived in Nazareth (Luke 1.26-27), travel to Bethlehem? Enter a Roman Emperor. Probably to replenish the imperial coffers he ordered an empire-wide census which involved people returning to their ancient family seat to register (Luke 2.1-3). So God used Augustus to bring about the fulfilment of Micah 5.2 (Prov 21.1), just as He provided in the Magi's gift of gold international currency to finance Mary and Joseph's flight to Egypt. Our God is in total control of history.

These are some lessons from the nativity. But note: "the arch-adversary of God has so planned his greatest travesty of the gospel that Christ should be largely represented to men as either in a cradle or on a cross" (W E Vine). Yes, a cutesy baby or a dying man - both sentimental, undemanding, unchallenging images. The gospel, however, proclaims with solemn dignity a risen, living, powerful Saviour in whom all authority is vested and before whom all men will one day bow. Nevertheless, even if we cannot surrender to the normal maudlin associations of Christmas, we can perhaps exploit the season to give our friends and unsaved relatives gifts (a Bible calendar, an evangelistic book) which may be used of God to make them think seriously about Him. And of course we can tell them the good news of what really happened and what it means (Luke 2.10-11). Think about it. And may the Lord grant you a specially blessed holiday season in which you can enjoy His grace.

Affectionately as always in Christ Jesus

WEEK THIRTY FOUR

Letter No 34:

Entering the New Year

As 2008 approaches I thought it might be fitting to write about what lies ahead. After all, this is a first time experience. You have never before entered a New Year with Christ as your Saviour – and that makes such a difference! Instead of facing the future in ignorance on your own, guided purely by your own preferences and the expectations of your social environment, you now belong to the greatest of masters who is Himself the Alpha and the Omega. Your destiny therefore lies safe in His hands. The next great event in God's prophetic calendar is what Christians often refer to as 'the rapture' (using the word in its sense of catching away). This will be the supernatural removal from the planet of all who belong to Christ to meet Him and resurrected believers in the air (1 Thess 4.13-18). And it may be that 2008 will be *the* year. However, whether it is or not (and scripture is silent about precise dating), it is our responsibility to live in the light of this glorious, certain hope. As Paul says, "we look for the Saviour" (Phil 3.20).

This of course is that time of year when people make resolutions to little real purpose. But it would be good to take on board the commitment, as the Lord enables you, to read right through His word during 2008, and perhaps make this an annual undertaking. Sadly, most believers appear to survive on scattered fragments of scripture instead of feasting on the wonderful variety of the whole counsel of God. I know you wish to get into the word, and I know too that, since God in His mercy saved you, you have been immersing yourself in the scriptures. This has been beautifully evidenced in your conversation and your prayers. Let me suggest seven principles to guide you in 2008.

First, we should read **regularly.** One of the pervasive biblical metaphors for God's word is food (Job 23.12; Psa 19.10b; 119.103; Jer 15.16; Matt 4.4).

This highlights several truths. Scripture is necessary (we cannot live without eating), tasty (let's face it, most of us enjoy eating) and demands a regular daily intake. After all, we cannot assimilate in one meal all the bodily sustenance we need for a whole week – little and often is the physical pattern the Creator has built into our digestive system. This therefore establishes the basic principle for Bible reading. A young fellow once suggested to me that taking a year out from work and setting himself to study the scriptures all day long would give him a thorough grounding in the word. Not so. As in nature, so in grace: we are to read and study habitually, not as an artificial academic discipline but as part of the essential fabric of our ordinary lives. That is why the local assembly, not a Bible College, is the biblical sphere for real spiritual growth and service. That way the word is always related to everyday experiences, fortifying us for our spiritual battle. The Israelites had to gather their manna on an individual daily basis, and so do we (Exod 16.21).

Second, we should read **systematically**. No one accidentally gets to know the Bible – it requires both diligence and method. There is, you see, always the danger that, unless I follow a clear comprehensive plan, I shall exclude from my schedule those portions which offend my prejudices. The Lord Jesus conspicuously included "every word" in His summary of the divine diet (Matt 4.4), just as Paul insisted that "all scripture" is profitable (2 Tim 3.16-17). Read the sad story in 2 Samuel 11 and 12 to see how King David remembered the minor law about sheep stealing in Exodus 22.1 (see 2 Sam 12.1-6), yet neglected the more important prohibition against murder (Exo 20.13). The unabbreviated word must fill our hearts. Now there are several good plans. The Choice Gleanings calendar takes you through the entire Bible in one year by giving you two portions of the Old and one of the New Testament each day. This involves quite a lot of reading. The TBS plan takes two years to get through the Bible with two readings a day, which means encountering the Psalms and New Testament twice. I have known people attempt a chronological rather than canonical order of reading, but this raises problems as there are differences of opinion as to, for example, where one places the books of Job and Joel. It is much simpler to follow the order of books in our Bible. However, it matters not which plan you use as long as you follow a system which guarantees you omit nothing.

Third, we must read **contextually**. Bible reading is not like dipping at random into a chocolate selection box, or listening to a CD of *Handel's Greatest Hits* as if that were his entire output. Although the Bible has been usefully divided into chapters and verses (and how valuable these are for reference purposes!) it was not all originally written that way. Therefore one best makes sense of, say, 1 Corinthians 13, by reading it immediately after chapter 12 and before chapter 14. This will throw new light upon a section all too frequently ripped from its moorings. Even individual words should be read in their context. I got into trouble the other Sunday by saying that Simon the Sorcerer in Acts 8.9-24 was not really saved at all. "Surely", said my questioner, "the inspired text says he believed?" Quite so – but every word must be read in the light of the scriptures as a whole. Does "believe" *always* means saving faith? Check with John 2.23-25 (an analogous passage about faith reliant on miracles), Luke 8.13 (which describes people who "for a while believe") and James 2.19. The New Testament does not have two words for faith – one meaning genuine God-given confidence in Christ, and the other false profession or mere mental assent. But the context determines: Simon's obsession with the miraculous and Peter's devastating response seem to place him in the latter camp. Real faith is always tested by time.

Fourth, we should try to read **objectively,** seeking to free ourselves from the presuppositions inevitably created by our upbringing, our cultural environment, and the often baleful influence of the established church. The understanding of much of the Bible's technical vocabulary has been contaminated by ecclesiastical tradition. For example, to many people "baptism" simply means infant sprinkling, "minister" conjures up a man in a dog-collar, while "bishop", "deacon" and "priest" refer to miscellaneous ecclesiastical dignitaries. Even the page headings in some printings of the AV are tainted by the assumption that Old Testament Israel is identified with the New Testament church. Above Zechariah chapter 9 in my TBS edition is written "God defendeth his church". Again, the "Reformed" notes on Zechariah 14.4 in the 1587 Geneva Bible read: "So that out of all the parts of the world, they will see Jerusalem…: and this he means of the spiritual Jerusalem the Church". But Zechariah is about Israel's future, and never mentions the church. We must always allow scripture to challenge our preconceptions and speak for itself.

Fifth, read **prayerfully.** Were Shakespeare alive he would doubtless put academics out of business by refuting their readings of his plays. But the author of the word is the Living God with whom we have constant contact by prayer. Just as the disciples went to the Lord for interpretive help (Matt 13.36), so can we, using the language of Psalm 119.18. And like Daniel, we can turn to prayer having read the word (Dan 9.2-4).

Sixth (and I am running out of space), read **sensitively** like the young King Josiah who was commended because he trembled at the word (2 Kings 22.10-11,18-19; Isa 66.1-2), for the Bible is no ordinary book. It is to be treated with due respect as the very voice of God.

Finally, we are to read **obediently**, seeking by grace to put into practice what we find in the word as God never reveals truth to satisfy mere intellectual curiosity (John 7.17; 13.17). There is always an obligation to obey (Deut 29.29). That's enough to keep both of us going through 2008! May the Lord feed and encourage your soul daily in His grace.

Affectionately as always in Christ Jesus

Letter No 35:

Blessings

You asked for a letter about blessing. Here it is – and I trust it will be as much a blessing to you as it has been to me in writing it! Back in the old days when I used to take young people's weekends, a lad came up and asked how it can be that God blesses us, but that we also bless Him. I cannot recall how I answered (badly, I suspect), but I could understand his bewilderment – the same word (whether in Hebrew or Greek) is used to describe both the divine action of providing benefits for men, and our responsive gratitude to God. For example, a careful reading of Matthew 26.26 (where the Lord Jesus "blessed and brake" the bread at supper) and its parallel in Luke 22.19 will show you how in certain contexts to bless obviously means to give thanks.

Perhaps the best place to start is Ephesians where both senses appear in the same verse: "Blessed *be* the God and Father of our Lord Jesus Christ, who hath blessed us with all spiritual blessings in heavenly *places* in Christ" (Eph 1.3). First of all then God is the great Blesser, for "without all contradiction the less is blessed of the better" (Heb 7.7). And His blessings may be divided into three kinds. In the first place there are the physical benefits He has showered upon the entire creation, for the God who made us also provided for us. Let us call these **creation blessings**:

> "So God created man in his *own* image, in the image of God created he him; male and female created he them. And God blessed them, and God said unto them, Be fruitful, and multiply, and replenish the earth, and subdue it: and have dominion over the fish of the sea, and over the fowl of the air, and over every living thing that moveth upon the earth. And God said, Behold, I have given you every herb bearing seed

... and every tree, in the which *is* the fruit of a tree yielding seed; to you it shall be for meat" (Gen 1.27-29).

These blessings include, to use Paul's words when preaching to pagans in Athens and Lystra, 'life, and breath, and all things' (Acts 17.25) such as 'rain from heaven, and fruitful seasons, filling our hearts with food and gladness' (Acts 14.17). Nor are they in any sense directed exclusively towards the regenerate – *all* creatures come into the good of them on the grounds of what theologians often call common grace, 'for he maketh his sun to rise on the evil and on the good, and sendeth rain on the just and on the unjust' (Matt 5.45). You see, our God is good even to rebellious sinners. The unsaved man is just as indebted to God as the believer for his life, his breath, his abilities and all he has, even though like Belshazzar he may be totally ungrateful: 'the God in whose hand thy breath *is*, and whose *are* all thy ways, hast thou not glorified' (Dan 5.23).

Then there are what I shall call **covenant blessings**. When in Genesis 12.1-3 God called Abraham to become the founding father of a unique nation with whom He would have a special relationship, He listed some of the associated benefits: "I will bless thee, and make thy name great; and thou shalt be a blessing: And I will bless them that bless thee, and curse him that curseth thee: and in thee shall all families of the earth be blessed". Of course, not all Abraham's natural descendants were saved, but they all enjoyed external covenant advantages as God's redeemed people. Paul itemizes some of these in Romans 9.4-5 as "the adoption [Israel was God's own son nation, set apart from others, as Amos 3.2 indicates], and the glory [the visible presence of God's glory in the overshadowing cloud of Exodus 16.10], and the covenants [particularly those with Abraham in Genesis 12, David in 2 Samuel 7, and the new covenant yet to be established with Israel in Jeremiah 31.31-37], and the giving of the law [the 10 commandments and the civil/ceremonial law of Exodus 20-23 etc], and the service *of God* [the tabernacle and temple worship], and the promises [of future prosperity under Messiah, such as Isaiah 2.1-5]; Whose *are* the fathers [the great men of Old Testament history], and of whom as concerning the flesh Christ *came*, who is over all, God blessed for ever" (Rom 9.4-5). Yes, Israel was given so much.

But what most concern us are **Christian blessings**, those wonderful divine provisions which uniquely single out believers of this era. Unlike creation blessings (which of course we also enjoy) these are primarily spiritual, irrevocably locked into the person and work of the Lord Jesus Christ. Just take time out to read through the first 14 verses of Ephesians 1, where some of them are catalogued. For example, we are chosen, predestined, adopted, accepted, redeemed, forgiven, and so on. This chapter, by the way, is a great antidote to spiritual depression or apathy because it so powerfully reminds us of what God in infinite grace has done for our souls through His beloved Son. When you feel low, that's where to go (pardon the rhyme!). And Paul conspicuously tells us that we have been blessed with "*every* spiritual blessing in the heavenlies in Christ" (J N Darby's translation). Note the significant "every". When you meet folk (and you will) who insist that you need a "second blessing" (by which they usually mean what are often called the charismatic gifts) to be a really spiritual Christian, just tell them that like all genuine saints of God you already have everything in Christ. And so you do.

Let's just pause here to note four simple facts. First, it is always God who takes the initiative in blessing. Genesis 1 is clear proof of that. Second, men are wholly dependent upon Him for everything they have, whether physical or spiritual, "for in him we live, and move, and have our being" (Acts 17.28). The usual Hebrew term for "bless" (Strong No 1288, and you can check all the words on your e-Sword) is said to come from a root meaning "to kneel", perhaps because this is the appropriate position for beggars receiving benefits. Third, all blessings are bestowed on the basis of sovereign grace: that is to say, we are altogether undeserving and God is under no obligation to any of us. Fourth (in case this isn't obvious) all blessings are for our ultimate good. Indeed, the word "blessed" (Strong No 833/5) used, for example, in Psalm 1.1 and 2.12, suggests the idea of happiness as the consequence of divine blessing. It is in fact translated "happy" in Deuteronomy 33.29. You may think this a mere quibble, but I incline to feel that "happy", derived originally from the noun "hap" (meaning chance, fortune, good luck), is not the most felicitous way of expressing a consciousness of divine favour. The happy man is the lucky man? No, we believe not in an arbitrary universe governed by luck but in the God who works "all things after the counsel of his own will" (Eph 1.11). What God gives us, including those adverse circumstances of life which may seem so incomprehensible and hard, is always best for us. As James 1.12 says, "Blessed is the man that endureth temptation". For that reason I think the word "blessed" (out of use in a secular world) well worth retaining.

But there is the other side. Those who recognize their utter indebtedness to God will respond with praise and thanks. The blessed thus become the blessers. No wonder the psalmist writes, "Bless the LORD, O my soul: and all that is within me, *bless* his holy name. Bless the LORD, O my soul, and forget not all his benefits" (Psa 103.1-2). Thereafter in verses 3 to 18 he rehearses some of his blessings, and in so doing instructs us in the art of praising God. To bless God is to recount all He is ("his holy name") and all He has done for us ("all his benefits"). For Christians this inevitably involves a special focus upon the final revelation of God in Christ (1 Pet 1.3-5). The common Greek word for bless is *eulogeo* (Strong No 2127) meaning literally "to speak well of". That is a good guide to our duty. When we bless God we speak well of Him and His Son. May that be our constant aim both in daily life and in those special corporate exercises of prayer and worship which we share with God's people.

Affectionately as always in Christ Jesus

WEEK THIRTY SIX

Letter No 36:

Gifts

I am slowly trying to work my way through your series of letter topics. This time it is GIFTS. Now I confess I was not quite sure what you had in mind here, but at this season of the year the word "gift" does at least have the merit of topicality. Since returning from darkest Devon I have been penning those "thank you" notes which are the expected response to Christmas presents. If I may digress, it always astonishes me how few people do that these days. A perfunctory grunt over the telephone is about all one can expect today by way of thanks. Now, when I was a boy (here's nostalgia for you!) we were brought up dutifully to acknowledge all gifts as soon as they were received: get a gift, write a note. This was impressed upon us as simple courtesy, and used to be the normal practice of both saved and unsaved. I recall an old Peanuts cartoon in which Lucy (she's the loud, bossy one) is complaining to her off-stage mom: "Do I *really* have to write thank-you letters for the toys I've already broken?" Well, yes, we do and we should. One of the rarer joys of dealing with youngsters is occasionally to find children who have been trained by their parents to respond personally, promptly and politely to their benefactors. It is lovely to be thanked. And there is something spiritually right about this. You see, one of the sad characteristics of fallen human beings is that they are discontented and unthankful (Rom 1.21); whereas Christians should of all people be constantly grateful to God for His mercy, and (by extension) to all others who may show them any kindness, however small. Goodness in men is but a faint glimpse of the goodness of God. In Matthew 10.42 a mere cup of cold water is registered as praiseworthy. Paul's epistle to the Philippians properly understood is an extended thank you letter, responding to the saints' practical thoughtfulness while the apostle was in a Roman prison (Phil 4.10-18). To adjust the language of 1 John 4.20, if we cannot be bothered to thank our fellow creatures for trivial acts of generosity, how can it be believed that we are truly grateful to the invisible

God for His innumerable daily benefits? In other words, gifts ought to provoke in the recipient a spirit of gratitude.

One of the first things we learn about God is that He is the great giver. "Behold, I have given you" (Gen 1.29), addressed to the newly formed Adam and Eve, can be written over the whole of the scriptures, because they testify to God's gracious, unfailing care for His creatures. Of ourselves we have nothing whatever "for we brought nothing into *this* world" (1 Tim 6.7). As we learned when investigating the subject of blessings, it is God who "giveth to all life, and breath, and all things" (Acts 17.25). More, "unto us a son is given" (Isa 9.6). The greatest of gifts is the only begotten Son, the Lord Jesus Himself, that "unspeakable gift" (2 Cor 9.15) with which Paul climaxes his two chapters specifically designed to stimulate Corinthian generosity towards their needy brethren. In modern English "unspeakable" unfortunately implies something too atrocious for words; whereas Paul's adjective, used only here in the New Testament, means that which is beyond the power of human expression. Words are inadequate to sum up the glories of Christ Jesus. Inextricably bound up with His wonderful person, of course, is the free gift of salvation, for "the gift of God is eternal life through Jesus Christ our Lord" (Rom 6.23). With that verse read John 4.10, Romans 5.15-18, and Ephesians 2.8-9. Our salvation from first to last is God's work– which is why it is so gloriously secure. A man who wished to join the fellowship of a company of believers in the USA was asked about his conversion. "Oh," said he, "I did my part, and God did His". Pressed to explain, he went on: "I did all the sinning and God did all the saving". Yes, I brought nothing whatever to my salvation apart from my sins. Just as the recipient does not contribute to his Christmas gift, so our salvation is entirely God's free grace gift to the totally undeserving.

But we can go further. The book of the Acts speaks about the "gift [singular]" of the Spirit (Acts 2.38; 8.20; 10.45; 11.17), clearly referring to the Holy Spirit Himself. In the early New Testament era there was occasionally a time gap between faith in Christ and the reception of the Spirit, but today at the very instant of conversion we receive the indwelling Spirit of God in all His fullness (1 Thess 4.8). Indeed, "if any man have not the Spirit of Christ, he is none of his" (Rom 8.9). Now, along with the Holy Spirit come those spiritual gifts about which Paul writes in 1 Corinthians chapters 12-14. While the actual phrase "the gifts of the Holy Ghost [Spirit]" appears only once (Heb 2.4), where it refers to the miraculous credential powers granted uniquely to the apostles (2 Cor 12.12), it can, I think, legitimately be used to describe the abilities given to believers for their Christian service. Let me attempt a definition. Spiritual gifts (and I use the phrase in the way it turns up in 1 Corinthians 12.1) are enablements given by God through the Holy Spirit to all believers so that they can effectively function in the body of Christ to the glory of His name. They facilitate the fulfilment of our spiritual responsibilities in the local assembly where God has placed us, because God never requires any duty without first giving the power to perform it.

1 Corinthians, the great New Testament instruction book on the local assembly, also makes it clear that we need spiritual graces (such as those listed in Galatians 5.22-23) properly to exercise spiritual gifts. This explains the significant placing of 1 Corinthians 13, with its surprising elevation of love above gift, for the possession of gift does not of itself guarantee godliness. The church at Corinth was possibly the most gifted in the New Testament, but it was also seriously damaged by carnality (1 Cor 1.7; 3.1). That is a vital lesson. Young men can all too easily be seduced by the glamour of platform ministry, as though that were the peak of spirituality. It is not. The most successful preacher in the Bible was tragically out of sympathy with God's heart. Read the book of Jonah and you will see what I mean. So never think that preaching the gospel or teaching the saints is an infallible index of achievement. It can, alas, become an ego-trip, for preachers are in constant danger of falling in love with the sound of their own voice. I freely confess I would love to see you so well established in the word that you are able, if the Lord will, to teach others; but it is more important that you become what the Lord wants you to be.

From Paul's teaching in 1 Corinthians 12 let me just list a few abiding principles for your consideration. Spiritual gifts are *spiritual* (12.1), not merely natural aptitudes (like athletic or artistic talents, although of course all these also are divinely given), and relate to the things of God. They are *familial* (12.1) in that they come with salvation: every child of God has at least one. Paul, for example, was obviously multi-gifted. They are *important* (12.1,3), because we need to be informed about them from the word. They are *Christ-honouring* (12.3), designed to glorify Him. They are *Trinitarian* (12.4-6), bestowed by the entire Godhead ("Spirit...Lord...God"). They are *varied* (12.4-6): just as the human body consists of different but equally vital functioning members, so does the body of Christ. After all, the one was created to illustrate the other. They are *harmonious* (12.4-6), given and controlled by the "same" divine Persons. They are wholly *unmerited* (12.4,7), because the word *charismata* means grace gifts. No servant of Christ can ever boast of his abilities. They are *profitable* (12.7), given not for personal satisfaction but for the benefit of all, although they are also *individual* (12.7,11), demanding personal responsibility for their exercise. They are *sovereign* (12.11), bestowed according to the will of God ("as he will") not man. We cannot just pick what we fancy. They are to be *regulated* (1 Cor 14.26,40) according to the instructions of the word, and exercised for spiritual edification in an orderly manner which honours the holy God who gave them.

These are of course just general principles. I cannot write here about the difference between the temporary gifts (like apostles, prophets, tongues) and the abiding gifts (evangelists, pastors, teachers, helps), for that requires a letter in itself. Nevertheless I hope I have given you something to think about. Keep growing in grace daily and you will find that, through the reading of the word, God will direct you into that sphere of service He has in mind for you. But be warned! Moses's training programme lasted some 80 years!

Affectionately as always in Christ Jesus

Letter No 37:

Matthew Chapter One

Since the New Year has now started in earnest you will probably, like me, be reading from Genesis, Job and Matthew. They make an outstanding combination as each book illuminates the others. Genesis confronts us initially with a good, sinless creation fresh from the hand of God, Job with a world under Satanic domination in which God nonetheless always effects His gracious purposes, and Matthew with the entrance into that fallen world of a perfect Saviour who would rescue His people. Just reading through this morning the following thoughts struck me from Matthew chapter one.

First, we can notice the **providence of God** in verses 1-17, for that introductory genealogy is by no means nugatory. As a boy I was once given an edition of the KJV which naughtily set in a smaller type face what the publishers considered insignificant portions of the scriptures, so they could easily be omitted in reading. But nothing in God's word is valueless. In a gospel specially dedicated to charting the fulfilment of Old Testament prophecy this detailed pedigree establishes the legal rights of the Lord Jesus Christ to the throne of Israel. The very first verse, with its echo of the structural formula found in the book of Genesis, highlights the fulfilment of two great Old Testament covenants: "The book of the generation of Jesus Christ, the son of David, the son of Abraham". To Abraham God promised a seed through whom the entire world would be blessed (Gen 12.1-3; 22.15-18), while to David He pledged that He would raise up to him a son to reign on Israel's throne (2 Sam 7.12-16). Although these promises had a short-term answer in Isaac and Solomon, both look beyond to the ultimate fulfilment in Christ (Gal 3.8-16; Acts 13.22-23). Thus two great themes in the divine programme for the world come together in Matthew chapter one: the kingdom theme, providing for righteous government through the ideal king, and the salvation theme, ensuring deliverance from bondage to sin. And nothing could thwart the accomplishment of God's plan – not even failure in the chosen people. Matthew amazingly mentions four women (not at all usual in genealogies) whose very names foreground failure: Tamar (incest), Rahab (prostitution), Ruth (from the enemy nation of Moab, Deut 23.3-6) and Bathsheba (adultery in the royal family). The nation sinned so badly that it was eventually judged by being carried way into Babylonian captivity (Matt 1.11) – yet still God's promises were sure. Not even my misdeeds can damage God's programme. Lesson: "our God *is* in the heavens: he hath done whatsoever he hath pleased" (Psa 115.3). What encouragement for us as we start a New Year!

Second, we might notice Matthew's **precision of language**. He is recording a genuine human birth, because the eternal Son of God truly took upon Himself sinless manhood, and yet he goes out of his way to signal that *this* birth was different from all others. The standard formula ("X begat Y") is suddenly interrupted when Joseph is reached: "Eliud begat Eleazar; and Eleazar begat Matthan; and Matthan begat Jacob; And Jacob begat Joseph the husband of Mary, of whom was born Jesus, who is called Christ" (1.15-16). This carefully preserves the virgin birth of the Lord Jesus: although Joseph was the legal father he had nothing to do with the child's conception. You might like to contrast Matthew 1.21 ("she shall bring forth a son, and thou shalt call his name Jesus") with Luke 1.13 ("thy wife Elisabeth shall bear thee a son, and thou shalt call his name John"), language which describes a normal human birth in which it is made clear to Zacharias that Elizabeth will bear *his* child. It is not surprising that the Lord Jesus emphasised the infallible linguistic details of the scriptures, validating even the tiniest jot and tittle (Matt 5.18). We can trust God's word implicitly!

Third, our chapter gives us in Joseph a superb **pattern of behaviour** under stress. Here is a godly man who suddenly discovers that his fiancée (they were not yet formally man and wife but were in the Jewish betrothal period) is pregnant. You can imagine his distress and confusion of mind, especially if she told him (as I assume she did) that this was a miraculous conception. How did he react? We read of his righteousness ("a just man", v.19), which means not that he was sinless but that relatively speaking he was an upright person (compare Luke 1.6). He therefore had a real concern for divine standards of conduct. By grace we have a righteous standing before God because of the work of Christ ("being justified by faith", Romans 5.1) but we are responsible also to live in a righteous manner day by day (1 John 3.10). Along with this integrity of character went gentleness: he was not prepared to subject Mary to a public humiliation by invoking the Old Testament law (such as Deuteronomy 22.23-24) against immorality. So he intended to divorce her quietly. It is all too possible to be unyieldingly strict and sour at the same time. But Joseph was tenderly considerate. Think of the very different behaviour of Claudio in *Much Ado about Nothing*. The Jews' words years later in John 8.41 suggest that rumours about the unusual circumstances of this pregnancy had spread, and therefore both Mary and Joseph would have suffered at the hands of scandalmongers. It is not pleasant to be misunderstood. Yet this they endured for the Lord's sake. Note also his thoughtfulness: "while he thought on these things" (1.20). One of the great features of Joseph is that he did not rush precipitately into action. Says the Proverb, "*He that is* slow to wrath *is* of great understanding: but *he that is* hasty of spirit exalteth folly" (14.29). That is good counsel in all situations – pause before you act and think things through carefully before the Lord. Many a sorrow might have been avoided had men stopped to ponder. And because Joseph took time to think he was therefore sensitive to the voice of the angel. Finally, he was scrupulously obedient: "Joseph being raised from sleep did as the angel of the Lord had bidden him" (1.24). May we be as loyal to the word.

Fourth, we have in verse 21 a marvellous **précis of God's salvation**: "thou shalt call his name JESUS: for he shall save his people from their sins". Yes, salvation is not so much an experience as a person. And that remarkable name (which means "Jehovah is Saviour") speaks of *a supernatural person*. Although there were men called Joshua (the Hebrew equivalent of Jesus) in Old Testament times, this one was unique because He truly combined in one person eternal deity and spotless humanity. He really was "God with us". Further, He would accomplish *a sure work*. "He shall save" – there was no possibility of failure, or of half measures. It is not that the Lord Jesus made salvation achievable, as though others then had to do something to complete it. No, "he shall save". This He would do for *a specific people*, "his people". Now this goes far beyond the boundaries of national Israel, although they are described in John's gospel as "his own [who] received him not" (John 1.11). John makes a sharp distinction between "his own" (the many) who rejected Him and "his own" (the few) whom He loved (John 13.1). You see, the Lord Jesus had a particular people, given to Him by the Father in eternity past (John 6.37; 17.6), drawn to Him irresistibly in time (John 6.44), a people who would hear His voice because they were His sheep (John 10.27). He would meet their deep *spiritual need*, delivering them not from physical oppression like Roman occupation but "from their sins". This implies rescue both from sin's eternal penalty and its present power (Gal 1.4).

How much we have to rejoice in – that God had mercy upon such sinful wretches as we are and provided in Christ Jesus a perfect salvation! May the Saviour guide and guard your steps through 2008.

Affectionately as always in Christ Jesus

Letter No 38:

The Christian and Death

Over the phone the other night you requested a letter to explain what the Bible says about death – so I am attempting this subject now. A rather grim topic, of course, but an unavoidable one. It is after all one of the most obvious facts of life in a fallen world. It was I think G B Shaw who said that the statistics of death were very impressive: one out of one dies! And the word of God pulls no punches. Biblical writers personify death as "the king of terrors" (Job 18.14), highlighting the effect it has on the ungodly, and the "last enemy" (1 Cor 15.26), because in God's programme it will finally be done away with so that in the new heaven and earth "there shall be no more death" (Revelation 21.4). I have concentrated here primarily on what death means to the believer. The position of the unsaved will require another letter.

First, death is a divinely-imposed **penalty**. This is clear when we read the account of man's sin in Genesis and the inspired commentary on it in Romans. God's warning to Adam about eating the fruit of the prohibited tree was very plain: "in the day that thou eatest thereof thou shalt surely die [lit., dying thou shalt die]" (Gen 2.17). And that is exactly what happened when he disobeyed: "by one man sin entered into the world, and death by sin; and so death passed upon all men, for that all sinned [that is, in Adam]" (Rom 5.12-14). Paul, you will note, does not treat Genesis as a collection of fanciful Middle Eastern legends but as historical truth. In other words, Adam's one act of rebellion brought all his posterity into condemnation so that every generation subsequently has come under the death penalty. William Tyndale's marginal note to the passage in his 1534 New Testament reads: "Adam's disobedience damned us all ere we ourselves wrought evil; and Christ's obedience saved us all, ere we ourselves work any good". Yes, I was condemned because of another's sin, and saved because of Another's righteousness. Of course, as well as this imputed guilt and the sin nature which I inherit from Adam I am also responsible for personal sins without number. Thus Paul speaks of the payment I fully deserve because of what I am and what I have done when he writes, "the wages of sin *is* death" (Rom 6.23). All this disposes of the comfortable secular fantasy of dying with dignity. All men are criminals in death row awaiting sentence from the righteous God who "killeth, and maketh alive: he bringeth down to the grave, and bringeth up" (1 Sam 2.6). Every physical death comes ultimately from God's hand, although He may use Satan as His instrument (Luke 12.5; Heb 2.14).

Second, death involves a **parting**. That is to say, it is not annihilation (as though those who die cease to exist) but a separation (of man from God, of soul from body). Godless men would be delighted were death simply everlasting unconsciousness. But it is not. That powerful word "perish" in John 3.16 means (as WE Vine puts it) "not extinction but ruin, loss, not of being, but of well-being". Aspects of death can be seen in the Genesis account of the Fall. First, Adam and Eve suffered immediate *spiritual death* once they ate the forbidden fruit, for the very act of disobedience ruined their fellowship with God. Instead of enjoying His company in the garden they hid, instinctively conscious of guilt and shame (Gen 3.7-8; John 3.19-20). This is what Paul means when he says that before salvation we were "dead in trespasses and sins" (Eph 2.1), "alienated from the life of God" (Eph 4.18). At the instant of conversion a miracle happens: "Even when we were dead in sins, [God] hath quickened us [made us alive] together with Christ, (by grace ye are saved;) And hath raised *us* up together, and made *us* sit together in heavenly *places* in Christ Jesus" (Eph 2.5-6). Second, Adam and Eve began to tend towards *physical death*, in that their perfect bodies were somehow changed under God's hand so as to contain the seeds of decay and dissolution, for "dust thou *art*, and unto dust shalt thou return" (Gen 3.19). Man became mortal. And when we trust Christ that does not change – believers' bodies still gravitate towards the grave, although of course the final instalment of our salvation lies ahead in "the redemption of our body" (Rom 8.23). This explains why believers, like others, suffer sickness and all the ills of life on a damaged planet culminating in physical death. Third, *eternal death*, endless exposure to God's burning wrath against sin in the lake of fire is, unless God's grace intervenes, the ultimate and irrevocable consequence of spiritual death (Rev 20.12-15). Never cease to be thankful to God for His great mercy in delivering you from that terrible destiny.

Third, for the believer in Christ death is simply a **portal** into the presence of the Lord Himself. The Saviour's death and resurrection have plucked the sting from death (1 Cor 15.56-57). Remember Herbert's marvellous poem "Death" which explores the difference Calvary has made. So what happens when a Christian dies? The body goes into the ground to "sleep" until resurrection. In both testaments death as far as the body is concerned is beautifully pictured as sleep (Dan 12.2; Matt 27.52; 1 Cor 15.51; 1 Thess 4.14-15), the metaphor implying the sure and glad hope of waking. When Stephen was stoned the narrative says "he fell asleep" (Acts 7.60), but immediately afterwards cuts ironically into the heart of Saul who was "consenting unto [not his sleep, with all its positive associations, but] his death" (8.1). When the Lord returns, the body that was laid in the grave will be raised up in power (1 Cor 15.42-49). On the other hand, the immaterial part, the soul and spirit, goes instantly and consciously into the glorious presence of the Saviour. Stephen knew that as he cried out, "Lord Jesus, receive my spirit" (Acts 7.59). The Lord had made a similar promise to the dying thief (Luke 23.43), but Paul gives the fullest exposition of this truth in 2 Corinthians 5 and Philippians 1, where he describes the blessedness of what we sometimes call "the intermediate state". Our current sin-damaged body is just like a tent, ready to be dismantled at the moment of death (2 Pet 1.14; 2 Cor 5.1). Until that moment, our condition in the world is summed up (using a neat little play on words) as "at home [*endemeo*] in the body . . . absent [*ekdemeo*, away from home] from the Lord". If, however, we pass through death, we are then "absent [*ekdemeo*, away from home] from the body, and . . . present [*endemeo*, at home] with the Lord" (2 Cor 5.6-8). Combining the teaching of 2 Corinthians 5 and Philippians 1.21-24 it is evident that this intermediate condition (between earthly life and the resurrection state) is both conscious and desirable ("at home with the Lord", "gain", "far better"). You will occasionally meet cults which teach the notion of "soul-sleep" (that at death the soul/spirit is unconscious until resurrection), but the Bible contains no support for it. Thus, although the process of dying may cause anxiety and distress death itself holds no horrors for the Christian. It leads into a condition far better than the best this life can offer.

Fourth – and this is thrilling – for the child of God death is only a **possibility**, not a certainty. Please note Paul's wonderful "if" in 2 Corinthians 5.1. You see, one generation of believers will not pass through death at all, for "we shall not all sleep" (1 Cor 15.51); rather, "we which are alive and remain unto the coming of the Lord . . . shall be caught up together with them [resurrected saints] in the clouds, to meet the Lord in the air" (1 Thess 4.15-17). It is the Lord's return (not death) which is held out as our great hope. Believers who have died are with the Lord but are "unclothed" (2 Cor 5.4) and still look forward eagerly to His coming when they, like us, will receive bodies eternally suited to their heavenly home. Dead and living saints are therefore both expecting the Saviour's coming – the only difference is that the former are in a better class of Waiting Room! May the Lord help us to keep waiting patiently for His Son from heaven (1 Thess 1.10).

Affectionately as always in Christ Jesus

Letter No 39:

The Pilgrim's Progress (v)

I think it's about time for yet another episode of *The Pilgrim's Progress*, my long-running opera (not soap, I hope, but spiritual), as there are yet more characters on the Christian pathway to meet. Remember: each of these dear folk reflects something we can probably see in ourselves, so there is much to learn. This is not designed to enable us to criticise others, but rather to challenge our own souls.

I do not know whether you have yet bumped into **Mr Doom and Gloom.** This is the brother, usually quite elderly, whose outlook seems always to be negative. Some folk almost enjoy looking on the black side. When Pooh and Piglet decide very thoughtfully to visit Eeyore the donkey he greets them with the discouraging query, "Lost your way, have you?" My mother used to describe an old lady in the London assembly of her childhood whose constant comment on life was, "It's all work, woe, and weariness". This was not calculated to encourage the saints. Sometimes of course the despondency stems from bitter personal experience. Poor Jacob reached a stage when, Joseph dead, Simeon imprisoned and now Benjamin about to be taken from him, he could see nothing ahead but misery: "And Jacob their father said unto them, Me have ye bereaved *of my children*: Joseph *is* not, and Simeon *is* not, and ye will take Benjamin *away*: all these things are against me" (Gen 42.36). But Jacob was wrong – he would in fact, in the good providence of God, see all his sons again. The New Testament antidote to such pessimism is Romans 8.31: "What shall we then say to these things? If God *be* for us, who *can be* against us?" Yes, one with God is a majority. And Jacob later came to realise this when he blessed his grandsons, "and said, God, before whom my fathers Abraham and Isaac did walk, the God which fed me all my life long unto this day, The Angel which redeemed me from all evil, bless the lads" (Gen 48.15-16). It is so healthy to acknowledge God's hand of blessing in our lives.

But then it is sometimes communal disappointment which fertilises a gloomy spirit. The older Israelites who recalled the glories of Solomon's temple could only weep at the poverty of its post-exilic counterpart:

> "And all the people shouted with a great shout, when they praised the LORD, because the foundation of the house of the LORD was laid. But many of the priests and Levites and chief of the fathers, *who were* ancient men, that had seen the first house, when the foundation of this house was laid before their eyes, wept with a loud voice" (Ezra 3.11-12; and compare Haggai 2.3).

It must have seemed so feeble compared with their glowing memories of past splendours. Certainly things in Great Britain have changed for the worse over the past half century. New Testament assemblies are not what they were. Even I can recall the time (in the 1950s) when the Gospel Hall of my childhood was packed out with people and the annual Sunday School treat involved the hiring of at least two double-decker buses to take the children to Wicksteed Park. And now the assembly, like so many others, is reduced to a handful of faithful believers. But we can never throw in the towel, or sit back to bemoan our failures. One of the greatest examples of determined personal godliness in a dark day is young King Josiah. He had every reason to blame the older generation and give up. After all, he was living at the fag end of Judah's kingdom, with Babylonian captivity looming. And yet he stood for God and influenced others for good (2 Kings 23.25). His whole story in 2 Kings and 2 Chronicles is worth reading. May we seek to strengthen, not enfeeble, God's people.

Quite a different character is **Mr Spring Up Overnight**. He is young, keen and remarkably advanced for his years. But does he have a real foundation to withstand the storms? In the parable of the sower, "some [seed] fell on stony ground, where it had not much earth; and immediately it sprang up, because it had no depth of earth: But when the sun was up, it was scorched; and because it had no root, it withered away". The Lord interprets thus: "these are they likewise which are sown on stony ground; who, when they have heard the word, immediately receive it with gladness; And have no root in themselves, and so endure but for a time: afterward, when affliction or persecution ariseth for the word's sake, immediately they are offended" (Mark 4.5-6,16-17). We might pause to notice that "affliction or persecution" is not a possibility but a certainty, for the Lord says "when", not "if". Now, the rocky ground hearer in the parable is not a true believer at all, but we can still learn from him. It is easy to ape spiritual maturity without being mature. I recall as a boy I used to bow my head (in simulated prayer) when I sat down in the meeting because I saw older folk doing it. But there is no neat, instant recipe for godliness; there is no substitute for solid progress in grace (Mark 4.28). We have to "take root downward" in order to "bear fruit upward" (2 Kings 19.30). Sudden and rapid growth is not always genuine. For example, John Mark started very well – in fact he accompanied Saul and Barnabas on their first missionary journey (Acts 13.1-5). But, alas, he soon departed from the work when things got hard, and was later the cause of division between two servants of God (Acts 13.13; 15.36-39). Perhaps he had been pushed forward too soon, for he was Barnabas's cousin. We should, I think, never promote our family (or those who are especially dear to us). Yet (and here's an encouragement) Mark came back, and significantly the same man who detected his failure later records his approval in 2 Timothy 4.10-11. Yes, the backslider can be restored.

Finally, look out for **Mr Slow and Steady**. There are many quiet, consistent believers who do not make great waves but keep on going in the right direction come rain or shine. I suppose I am thinking of the fable of the hare and the tortoise – the one starting with a tremendous burst of energy but falling into sleepy complacency, the other simply plodding away. Mr Plod, you may remember, was the rotund, slightly comic policeman in the Noddy books. But to be honest, that is the best any of us can do spiritually – *just plod on for God*. Most of the Christian life, you will already have realised, is not a spiritual mountain top. The crowds at your baptismal service have all faded away and the assembly has dwindled back to its normal size. But you have to carry on day by day. Timothy is the pattern. He was young (1 Tim 4.12), diffident (1 Tim 4.14-16; 2 Tim 1.6,14), tender-hearted (2 Tim 1.4), and not in the best of physical health (1 Tim 5.23). But Paul's word to him, placed in the solemn context of surrounding failure and unfaithfulness, applies to all: "evil men and seducers shall wax worse and worse, deceiving, and being deceived. But continue thou in the things which thou hast learned and hast been assured of" (2 Tim 3.14). "Continue thou". That's the challenge. My friends may fail, gospel testimony may become even weaker, the world around will assuredly drift further and further away from the truth of God, but I must, by God's grace, go on. And that is what I would have you do. There are tough times ahead, for the New Testament leaves us in no doubt about the increase of godlessness in the last days. But God is enough for all your needs. The best I can do then is to "commend you to God, and to the word of his grace, which is able to build you up, and to give you an inheritance among all them which are sanctified" (Acts 20.32). And that I do, daily. So just keep on. As a friend of mine puts it, "Go slow, keep low, and don't blow".

Affectionately as always in Christ Jesus

Letter No 40:

Genesis 22

I confess I find it is always exhilarating to reread Genesis, Job and Matthew at the start of the New Year– each book is so spiritually rich and yet also so very different. The seed plot of Genesis fertilises the rest of the scriptures (by introducing us to a range of fundamental truths such as creation, the origin of sin and death, the meaning of sacrifice, faith, divine judgment, and God's sovereign call), whereas the poetry of Job gets deep into the heart of human experience in a ruined world, while Matthew methodically explores the earthly ministry of the long-expected Messiah, assiduously noting the fulfilment of Old Testament prophecy.

The other day the story of Abraham's sacrifice in Genesis 22 struck me afresh. The chapter is packed full of spiritual nourishment. First of all, we have in both Abraham and Isaac a **pattern of godly behaviour.** Abraham's instant alertness to the voice of God is impressive (v.1). Would that we were as quick to hear the word! But even more challenging is his astonishing obedience to such an unexpected and costly command (vv.2-3). Remember that Isaac was no ordinary son. Beyond all human expectation, he had been born as the result of a divine prediction when his mother was 90 and his father 100, and was the subject of special promises which announced blessing for the entire planet (Gen 12.1-3; 15.4-5; 17.5-8). In other words, all Abraham's hopes were centred in this child ("whom thou lovest") – and now the same God who gave him asked for him back. Abraham obeyed without question, without complaint, without delay, anticipating the language of the Psalmist in 119.60, and the confession of Job 1.21. The stark scriptural narrative does not probe into his thoughts, merely recording his actions – yet behind them all we can imagine the pangs of his heart. And his sorrow must have continued over three long days, for he had to travel quite a distance with Isaac to the place of sacrifice, during which time he was always conscious of what lay ahead (v.4). Yet on reaching Moriah his words to the accompanying servants are all the more amazing: "Abide ye here with the ass; and I and the lad will go yonder and worship, and come again to you" (v.5). Both would go and worship; both would return. What faith! The writer to the Hebrews provides the commentary:

> "By faith Abraham, when he was tried, offered up Isaac: and he that had received the promises offered up his only begotten *son*, Of whom it was said, That in Isaac shall thy seed be called: Accounting that God *was* able to raise *him* up, even from the dead; from whence also he received him in a figure" (Heb 11.17-19).

Although Genesis does not spell this out, Abraham believed that the God who had promised universal benefits through Isaac would have to raise Isaac from the dead to fulfil His word. Bear in mind that (i) in human history there had been no prior example of a resurrection, (ii) the doctrine of resurrection had not yet been revealed, and (iii) burnt offering involved reducing the victim to ashes, ashes which on the top of a wind-swept mountain would have been instantly dispersed into the atmosphere. Still Abraham was convinced that he and his son would come back down from the mountain. Here's a man who trusted God's promise.

But notice too that Isaac did not object. We are not told his exact age, but Jewish tradition places him in his early twenties. Certainly he was old enough to do the heavy work for Abraham (v.6). Now, the relationship between this father and son is a model of mutual confidence and respect (vv.6-8). That Abraham had taught him the things of God is evident in Isaac's knowledge about worship and burnt offerings. It is in the home that godly training begins (Prov 22.6); Abraham had obviously fulfilled the Lord's expectations of him (Gen 18.17-19). Further, as a good father should be, he was on hand to answer his son's practical inquiry: "Here I am, my son" (v.7). His response to a question he must have dreaded, one which chilled his heart, is a combination of resignation and unconscious insight: "God will provide himself a lamb for a burnt offering". The ambiguity is profound: God would indeed eventually provide a lamb, but one who was equal with Himself (John 1.29). The actual substitute for Isaac was no lamb but a full-grown ram caught by the very emblem of its adult strength, its horns. Abraham's answer therefore looked beyond the present across the centuries to the arrival of God's Lamb, Christ Jesus. And although the young man would doubtless have been physically able to resist his father's intentions had he so wished, it appears he allowed himself to be bound and laid on the altar (one he presumably helped to build). The Pauline instruction, "Children, obey *your* parents in all things: for this is well pleasing unto the Lord" (Col 3.20), is here marvellously exemplified.

Second, the chapter is **a picture of Calvary**. Of course, every Old Testament sacrifice in some measure looks forward to the ultimate offering (Eph 5.2), but this one is particularly memorable. It illustrates the Father's eternal love for the Son (v.2; Matt 3.17; Rom 8.32), the unimpeded fellowship of Father and Son in our redemption, for "they went both of them together" (vv.6,8; see John 8.29; 16.32), and the Son's total submission to the Father's will (v.9; John 4.34; 13.1). Scripture traces salvation to the Father who "loved and gave" (John 3.16) and to the Son "who loved me and gave himself for me" (Gal 2.20). Further, this sacrifice acts out the idea of substitution in the sudden provision of a replacement for Isaac (vv.13; 1 Pet 3.18; Isa 53.6). *En route* to Moriah Isaac typifies the Lord Jesus, but as delivered from death he also represents folk like us, saved by the death of another. Thus the slain ram speaks momentarily of the Saviour. Even the site has significance in that it eventually became the location of Solomon's temple (2 Chron 3.1). Finally, although no literal resurrection took place, it is there "in a figure" (Heb 11.19), since Isaac's eleventh-hour rescue must have seemed like life from the dead.

Third, we are instructed in basic **principles of the Christian life**. The chapter starts with the solemn truth that God tests His people, not to expose their failure but to bring out their faith (vv.1,12; James 1.12). And the toughest testing may come at the end of the journey: "after these things" (v.1) reminds us that Abraham had already been through much and was now advanced in years. There is no easy retirement in the pilgrim life. Many dear elderly saints face more difficulties than we can ever know. Then we learn that worship is no thoughtless, casual ritual but the exercise of a prepared heart, requiring much of the worshipper (vv.2-3). We can only offer to God what has cost us time and effort in the spiritual study of the word. Abraham's obedience to an order that flew in the face of all God had previously said to him offers a master class in how to react to apparent contradictions in scripture. Our responsibility to God's word is simple: (i) to obey its precepts and (ii) to believe its promises, even when they seem at loggerheads. The believer's business is to obey and leave the consequences with God. More, it is in the severest trials that we discover new glories in our God. Stripped (potentially) of all that was dear to him, Abraham found that the Lord would provide (vv.8,14). For the first time in scripture God is known as Jehovah-Jireh. As someone puts it, "when we are brought to the place where Christ is all we have, we shall discover that Christ is all we need". Easy to write, but hard to experience. Nevertheless, Abraham's faith was divinely acknowledged and appreciated. Far from rescinding His promises, God elaborated and confirmed them with an oath (vv.15-18). We never lose out by believing our God – so keep trusting.

Affectionately as always in Christ Jesus

Letter No 41:

Romans Chapter One

Thanks for your visit the other night. I much enjoyed having a glance through the introductory paragraph of Romans chapter one with you. Paul's prologues are never to be overlooked as they usually provide vital information about the letter as a whole, and this one is especially fascinating as Romans is the definitive biblical exposition of the gospel.

I thought I'd just sum up some of the things we discovered from verses 1-17. We can structure the section around those seven crucial "of God" phrases which I pointed out to you. Since the gospel is from the start specifically called "**the gospel of God**" (v.1), we have a clear testimony to its impeccable authority and its total credibility. What comes from God is stamped with the authority of heaven itself and must be as trustworthy as the God who "cannot lie" (Tit 1.2). This provides us with unshakable assurance (as we are not depending for our soul's salvation upon the untruths, the mistakes or the wishful thinking of men) and simultaneously with the grandest of responsibilities, for to communicate such a message to others requires that we pass it on unabridged, unelaborated and unchanged. You drew my attention to the faithfulness of Abraham's servant in Genesis 24, a man who was not at liberty to adjust his commission in order to indulge his hearers. Similarly, the gospel preacher (or the individual believer seeking to tell his friends about the Saviour) cannot alter the terms of the good news. Saving people, you see, is God's sovereign privilege; telling them the message accurately is ours.

But if 'gospel of God' spells out the supernatural source of the news, "**Son of God**" (v.4) highlights its subject. Now this is worth emphasising. The gospel is not primarily about you and me, although of course by grace we may benefit from it. Sinful man loves to be at the centre of things, either as hero or as victim; that is why some people are so hotly opposed to the very notion that there is a God before whom they must one day bow. But God's good news is about His Son for it casts the spotlight upon the most glorious person in the universe – the one in whom, through whom, and for whom the entire creation was made (Col 1.15-17). In all things, even in the proclamation of deliverance from sin, He must have the pre-eminence (Col 1.18). In case we are in any doubt, the meaning of "Son of God" is best seen by observing how the Lord's unsympathetic contemporaries understood it (John 5.18; 19.7). Not for them any of the Jehovah's Witnesses' nonsense about an exalted angelic being; no, they grasped that Jesus of Nazareth was claiming absolute equality with God. And He, always prompt to put His disciples right when they erred and expose the inconsistencies of the religious leaders, never corrected their understanding. Rather than simply referring to Jesus, Paul therefore gives the Lord a title underlining His deity for, as an Anglican bishop once said, "a Saviour not quite God is a bridge broken at the farther end". He who came to save us became man that He might die, but He remained eternally God for His death to have infinite value.

"**Beloved of God**" (v.7) introduces the people in Rome who had already come into the good of this gospel. The phrase is qualified by what follows: "called to be saints". Here were folk, probably considered nonentities by the Roman social and political elite, who were (i) specially beloved of God, and (ii) called to be His set-apart people in the world, people marked by a holiness of life-style which reflected something of the character of God Himself. Now you may say, surely God loves the whole world? Well, the crux verse (John 3.16) interestingly puts this love in the past tense: "God so loved the world that He gave". In other words, God's love has been demonstrated historically in the giving of Christ Jesus so that each one who trusts in Him receives eternal life. But rebel sinners have no right to bask in the sunshine of God's love, as though this were some unconditional guarantee of safety, until they bow to His command and obey the gospel. Then and only then do they come practically and personally into the enjoyment of God's affections. Although the book of the Acts is the inspired narrative of New Testament gospel preaching nowhere that I can see, apart from 15.25 (which describes two believers), does it mention the word "love". Peter and Paul faithfully preached sin, grace, Christ, the cross, repentance and faith, but they are not recorded as majoring in God's love. There is nothing sentimental or saccharine about their evangelism. The gospel is not a cosy invitation but a solemn command. When the rich young ruler (Mark 10.17-22) turned sorrowfully away, his bosom sin exposed by the Saviour's words, the Lord (who as

Mark tells us, "loved him") did not pursue him with the exhortation, "Smile, God loves you!" No, until we recognize and confess our utter ruin before God we can never appreciate the true meaning of His love in providing at such cost a Saviour. John's first letter informs us that "God is light" (1.5) before ever it tells us that "God is love" (4.8). You see, although God goes out in kindness to all (Matt 5.44-45) it is for His own that He has a special and eternal love which results in their salvation (Jer 31.3; John 13.1; Eph 5.25). No wonder we love Him (I John 4.19)!

"**The will of God**" (v.10) moves us into the second main function of Paul's prologue – to explain why he had not yet visited Rome (vv.9-15). He had purposed to see them, he was currently praying that the Lord would enable him to do so, but all his petitions were conditional upon God's will. In a world which on the surface seems to be dominated by man's will it is encouraging to see behind the scenes that God is infallibly working out His purpose. To hedge our prayers with the proviso "if it be Thy will" is no cop-out but humble submission to a God who knows best. The first miracle in Matthew (Matt 8.1-4) is a superb demonstration. A leper approaches the Saviour in an attitude of worship, with an ascription of deity on his lips ("Lord") and a confession of implicit confidence in the Lord's power ("thou canst make me clean"), while simultaneously bowing to His sovereign will ("if thou wilt"). That's a model for our prayers. Later, Romans chapters 9-11 expound something of God's will in relation to the nation of Israel and the provision of salvation ("therefore hath he mercy on whom he will *have mercy*, and whom he will he hardeneth", 9.18). How reverent we should be in our thoughts about such a great God!

"**The power of God**" (v.16) is the divine energy source in the gospel. No other message is instinct with dynamism to change lives for good. The power of God unto judgment was seen at Babel, at the flood, at the destruction of Sodom and Gomorrah, and will be seen in the future when the vials of God's wrath are poured out upon a Christ-rejecting planet (Rev 6-19). But the good news announces that this same God has "power unto salvation" to each one who believes. Every genuine conversion is a miracle of divine transformation (2 Cor 5.17).

But "**the righteousness of God**" (v.17) reminds us that salvation by no means minimises God's holy standards. On the contrary, the glory of the gospel is that what God's righteousness demanded (perfection of life, or the death sentence) His love has provided (in that the Lord Jesus lived a sinless life and then "offered himself without spot to God", Heb 9.14). An old hymn puts it well:

> The love of God is *righteous* love,
> Seen in Christ's death upon the tree;
> Love that exacts the sinner's debt,
> Yet, in exacting, sets him free.

The gospel wonderfully enables God to be "just and the justifier of him which believeth in Jesus" (Rom 3.26).

Finally, **"the wrath of God"** (v.18) reveals God's holy anger against sin. Wrath is present right now in the built-in consequences of sinful behaviour (1.18-32), but its full manifestation awaits the future (2.5-6; Rev 6.15-17). We should never cease to be thankful that we are "not appointed unto wrath" but to obtain the final instalment of salvation at Christ's return (1 Thess 5.9-10). May that assurance encourage you to continue daily in grace.

Affectionately as always in Christ Jesus

Letter No 42:

Shepherds

I thought I'd jot down a few thoughts today on the subject of shepherding, since it is so important throughout the Bible. It illustrates both the ministry of the Lord Jesus Christ for His people (John 10.11; Heb 13.20; 1 Pet 5.4), and the service of local assembly elders in taking care of the spiritual requirements of the believers for whom the Lord has given them a responsibility (Acts 20.28). You will probably recall (as it was in Choice Gleanings recently!) how the Lord Jesus highlights the difference between secular and spiritual leadership: "Ye know that the princes of the Gentiles exercise dominion over them, and they that are great exercise authority upon them. But it shall not be so among you: but whosoever will be great among you, let him be your minister" (Matt 20.25-26). In other words, true leaders serve.

The scriptural model of leadership is therefore neither tyrannical (cruel domination) nor managerial (detached administration) but pastoral. In the Old Testament the shepherd is a remarkable picture of God's ideal of kingship. And of course God Himself marvellously sets the pattern (Psa 23.1). Instead of the power-hungry, egotistical potentate, God's provision for His people Israel was an active, selfless, caring benefactor. It is therefore not surprising that, for example, Moses received his training for leading an entire nation through the wilderness while feeding the flock of Midian in the desert, or that David was taken from tending his father's sheep in order to nurse God's flock (Psa 80.1). Both were called by God to protect and guide His people:

> "Thou leddest thy people like a flock by the hand of Moses and Aaron…He chose David also his servant, and took him from the sheepfolds: From following the ewes great with young he brought him to feed Jacob his people, and Israel his inheritance. So he fed them according to the integrity of his heart;

and guided them by the skilfulness of his hands" (Psa 77.20; 78.70-72).

Let me list some characteristics of the ideal shepherd. We can see them illustrated in Jacob's faithful service for his uncle Laban.

> "This twenty years *have* I *been* with thee; thy ewes and thy she goats have not cast their young, and the rams of thy flock have I not eaten. That which was torn *of beasts* I brought not unto thee; I bare the loss of it; of my hand didst thou require it, *whether* stolen by day, or stolen by night. *Thus* I was; in the day the drought consumed me, and the frost by night; and my sleep departed from mine eyes. Thus have I been twenty years in thy house; I served thee fourteen years for thy two daughters, and six years for thy cattle: and thou hast changed my wages ten times. Except the God of my father, the God of Abraham, and the fear of Isaac, had been with me, surely thou hadst sent me away now empty. God hath seen mine affliction and the labour of my hands, and rebuked *thee* yesternight" (Gen 31.38-42).

First of all the true shepherd must be **resident** with the flock. Jacob could not do his job from a distance. Come wind and weather he had to be on the spot ("with thee") where he was needed. That is why Peter speaks of elders being "among" the saints in a local assembly (1 Pet 5.1). It is impossible simultaneously to be a local church elder and a travelling circuit preacher. As a consequence, the godly elder will never become famous down here because his sphere of activity is restricted. But he will gain God's approval, which is all that matters (1 Pet 5.4).

Second, the shepherd is **persistent** in his work ("thus have I been twenty years in thy house"), as his is no short-term service. He cannot run off to pastures new, he cannot accept other offers, but must stick doggedly to his task even though the numbers with whom he works be small. David's brothers jeered about "those few sheep" (1 Sam 17.28), but we must remember that in God's eyes numbers are not everything. A mere eight were saved in the ark, yet Noah is not criticised for failure. What God looks for is not success (which after all is His business) but faithfulness "in a very little" (Luke 19.17).

Further, the shepherd must be **vigilant**, his eye constantly alert to the specific needs of the flock. Jacob obviously paid scrupulous attention to "thy ewes and thy she-goats" at lambing time, when urgent assistance might well be required. Individual sheep may stray, or contract disease, or be wounded by the attacks of predators. In one of the great shepherding chapters of the Old Testament (Ezekiel 34) God charges the religious leaders of the nation with negligence in their duty: "The diseased have ye not strengthened, neither have ye healed that which was sick, neither have ye bound up *that which was* broken, neither have ye brought again that which was driven away, neither have ye sought that which was lost; but with force and with cruelty have ye ruled them" (v.4). Invert that verse and you have a description of everything a true elder should be doing: watching carefully over the flock, providing encouragement, correction and guidance where needed.

Fourth, godly shepherding is **unselfish** ("the rams of thy flock have I not eaten"). The shepherd is not self-serving, not ministering "for filthy lucre, but of a ready mind" (1 Pet 5.2). In other words, he is not in it for personal gain, self-esteem, or the pleasure of power. His loyalty is unswervingly to his Master, whose sheep he tends, for each local assembly is "the flock of God" (1 Pet 5.2).

Fifth, shepherd work is personally **costly**. Says Jacob, "*Thus* I was; in the day the drought consumed me, and the frost by night; and my sleep departed from mine eyes". It is relatively easy to visit an assembly for a series of special meetings: you receive the adulation reserved for a celebrity and are not there long enough for the saints to discover what you are really like. I speak as one who knows! But to stick faithfully to one little company of believers, and try by God's grace to serve day in day out, amid criticism, disappointment and weakness, is tough. Someone has said that an elder requires the love of a mother, the wisdom of a father, and the skin of a rhinoceros. I recall an elder in my student days who could not sleep at nights, so burdened was he about the state of the assembly in which God had placed him.

Sixth, it is a **tender** work. God's sheep and lambs are to be fed and tended (John 21.15-17), not bullied. That is why one of the qualifications of an elder is that he be "apt [able] to teach" the word (1 Tim 3.2), both, I think, on the platform and in the home. He will demonstrate a kind-hearted concern for the needy individual as well as the whole company. And the ability to do that comes neither automatically nor easily – long hours are spent in the study before one can teach the saints. I can think of godly men who spent time and effort helping me in my younger days.

Finally, it is an **exemplary** work: that is, elders must be a pattern of what they teach, for biblical shepherds (unlike their western counterparts) lead from the front rather than drive from the rear, being not "lords over *God's* heritage, but...ensamples to the flock" (1 Pet 5.3; Psa 23.2-3; Isa 40.11; John 10.3-4). One final point: no one could do such exhausting work without divine aid. Thus Jacob: "except the God of my father, the God of Abraham, and the fear of Isaac, had been with me..." Divine work demands divine strength, and God graciously supports His people as they serve Him.

But what of the responsibility of the sheep to their shepherds? Ever since you entered the Coatbridge assembly you have experienced pastoral care because an elder has gone out of his way to take an interest in you. I am sure you will remember to thank God for him, to pray for him, and seek to encourage him in turn – he will appreciate it (Heb 13.7,17).

Affectionately as always in Christ Jesus

Letter No 43:

Lessons from Joseph

Like me you will probably at the moment be reading through the fascinating life of Joseph in the latter part of Genesis. The space devoted to just one man is remarkable in a book which includes an account of creation and the first few thousand years of the earth's history– but then Joseph is a special case. Biblical biography is always full of lessons, for "whatsoever things were written aforetime were written for our learning, that we through patience and comfort of the scriptures might have hope" (Rom 15.4). Among other things, he illustrates (i) the providential hand of God directing the steps of His people, (ii) the great principle of God's educational programme, that suffering precedes glory, and (iii) aspects of the person and work of the Lord Jesus Christ.

What can we learn about God from Joseph's life? One method is to examine the way he refers to the Lord in his conversation. Now Joseph is in no sense preaching on the doctrine of God; yet his talk is always informative. The way we mention God is in itself a testimony to what we understand of Him. That is why we should speak of Him with due reverence and caution. The first occasion in the biblical record that Joseph takes the Lord on his lips is while he is a slave in Egypt, serving Potiphar. Don't overlook the context: despite those amazing prophetic dreams of future exaltation (Gen 37.6-9) he was now rejected by his own brothers and captive in a far country. What hope was there of rescue or reunion? Yet his first mention of God is not coloured by bitterness or cynicism. Tempted by the seductive Mrs Potiphar he responds with an affirmation of steadfast loyalty to the **God of holiness**: "how then can I do this great wickedness, and sin against God?" (Gen 39.9) His present adverse circumstances did not cloud his understanding of God's standards: even away from his own home, he must obey God rather than men. Indeed, as the story goes on, he takes to his heels to escape peril, embodying the truth Paul later taught Timothy: "flee also youthful lusts" (2 Tim 2.22). Because God is holy (that is, completely set apart from all that is sinful and defiled) so must His people be (1 Pet 1.15-16). Second, he recognizes the **God of knowledge**. His personal integrity seems only to have led to further humiliation, and he is now in prison. And yet when those whom he serves speak of dreams he is quick to direct them to his God: "*Do* not interpretations *belong* to God?" (Gen 40.8). Our God is "a God of knowledge, and by him actions are weighed" (1 Sam 2.3), for nothing can be hid from His all-seeing eyes. When we do not know which way to turn, we can turn to the One who understands all. Third, Joseph knew that his was a **God of grace**. When two years later Pharaoh experiences mysterious, foreboding dreams, and the Chief Butler suddenly recollects the young man who had so encouraged him in prison, Joseph is quick to deny any personal ability. Instead he testifies to God's kindness to the undeserving: "Joseph answered Pharaoh, saying, *It is* not in me: God shall give Pharaoh an answer of peace" (Gen 41.16).

Fourth, God is a **God of revelation**, for "God hath shewed Pharaoh what he *is* about to do" (Gen 41.25). The crucial question "Canst thou by searching find out God? canst thou find out the Almighty unto perfection? *It is* as high as heaven; what canst thou do? deeper than hell; what canst thou know?" (Job 11.7-8) of course assumes the answer "No". God is totally inaccessible to His creatures – unless, that is, He chooses to make Himself known. And this is the great wonder of the Bible. Far from being, as some think, a record of man's speculations about God, it is God's infallible revelation of Himself. And that revelation includes inerrant information about past (Gen 1.1), present and future (John 16.13; Rev 1.1). But, fifth, God is also the **God of action**: "What God *is* about to do he sheweth unto Pharaoh" (Gen 41.28). No mere looker-on in the affairs of men, God is fully involved in the world He has made. Although the natural man cannot see His hand at work, the believer is alert to divine working even in what we might call the secular sphere. Whatever the results of a forthcoming American election we can be certain of this: "the most High ruleth in the kingdom of men, and giveth it to whomsoever he will, and setteth up over it the basest of men" (Dan 4.17). Sixth, he is the **God of unthwartable purpose**: "the thing *is* established by God, and God will shortly bring it to pass" (Gen 41.32). After all, "he doeth according to his will in the army of heaven, and *among* the inhabitants of the earth: and none can stay his hand, or say unto him, What doest thou?" (Dan 4.35) It matters not what men or angels may do, He will fulfil His will – which means that His purpose to glorify worthless folks like you and me cannot fail (Rom 8.28-31)!

More, He is the **God of forgetfulness**, in the sense that He tenderly erases from His people the memory of sorrow. As Joseph says, enraptured at the birth of his first son, "God, *said he*, hath made me forget all my toil, and all my father's house" (Gen 41.51). I believe that in heaven the painful recollection of our own failures and afflictions down here will be replaced by the sheer delight of being in the glory, "for God shall wipe away all tears from their eyes; and there shall be no more death, neither sorrow, nor crying, neither shall there be any more pain: for the former things are passed away" (Rev 21.4). Joseph's second son Ephraim provoked another comment: "for God hath caused me to be fruitful in the land of my affliction" (Gen 41.52). The **God of fruitfulness** cultivates in His people those godly characteristics of (for example) endurance, love, holiness which bring Him pleasure, for "herein is my Father glorified, that ye bear much fruit; so shall ye be my disciples" (John 15.8). And such fruit is often best produced in the soil of trials and difficulty, for "tribulation worketh patience; And patience, experience; and experience, hope: And hope maketh not ashamed; because the love of God is shed abroad in our hearts" (Rom 5.3-5). We must never forget that all our circumstances are ordered by God so that we might grow in grace to His glory. To the young believer who, under the pressure of severe distress, exclaimed, "I wish I'd never been made", a wiser friend replied, "You're not – you are *being* made". Faith brings us into spiritual life, but trials develop our spiritual muscles. At the same time, an experience of God's mercy should never dilute our appreciation of His magnificence. When his brothers turn up in Egypt seeking food to sustain them through the famine Joseph says, "I fear God" (Gen 42.18), for ours is the **God of awesome majesty**. The privilege of salvation should never rob us of reverence for His infinite greatness (Heb 12.28-29).

Finally, when he at last reveals himself to his brothers, Joseph comes out with the first great biblical statement of God's overruling power:

> "I *am* Joseph your brother, whom ye sold into Egypt. Now therefore be not grieved, nor angry with yourselves, that ye sold me hither: for God did send me before you to preserve life. For these two years *hath* the famine *been* in the land: and yet *there are* five years, in the which *there shall* neither *be* earing nor harvest. And God sent me before you to preserve you a

posterity in the earth, and to save your lives by a great deliverance. So now *it was* not you *that* sent me hither, but God" (Gen 45.4-8; 50.20).

Ours is the **God of providence.** His brothers may have sold him, but it was God who sent him into Egypt for the purpose of bringing blessing to those who hated him! One thinks of Acts 2.23. Our God is in sovereign control of all – great cause for rejoicing, for we cannot be in safer hands.

Affectionately as always in Christ Jesus

Letter No 44:

Israel and the Church

I mentioned the other night that I would attempt a letter on the difference between Israel and the church as this is an area where many believers seem to make unwarranted assumptions, assumptions based largely one feels on tradition rather than an inductive study of scripture. You have already noticed Matthew Henry's tendency to identify the two. The confusion is an old one. It is sometimes called supersessionism (because the church is thought to have superseded Israel) or replacement theology (because the church has replaced Israel in God's programme).

Now it is indeed true that just as Israel was God's people in the Old Testament so the church is God's people in the present age. It is also true that there are parallels between God's Old Testament and His New Testament people. The history of Israel illustrates the experience of believers, and is full of lessons for us (1 Corinthians 10.1-11). But similarity must not be mistaken for sameness. The man who confuses a Rolls Royce with a mini because they both have four wheels is not likely to get top marks for observation! To equate Israel and the church effectively transfers wholesale all the great Old Testament promises from the nation to the spiritual people of God today. Thus, according to Matthew Henry, Isaiah 2 (just to take a random example) describes "the setting up of the Christian church, and the planting of the Christian religion, in the world". But what does Isaiah actually say?

> "The word that Isaiah the son of Amoz saw concerning Judah and Jerusalem. And it shall come to pass in the last days, *that* the mountain of the LORD'S house shall be established in the top of the mountains, and shall be exalted above the hills; and all nations shall flow unto it. And many people shall go

and say, Come ye, and let us go up to the mountain of the LORD, to the house of the God of Jacob; and he will teach us of his ways, and we will walk in his paths: for out of Zion shall go forth the law, and the word of the LORD from Jerusalem. And he shall judge among the nations, and shall rebuke many people: and they shall beat their swords into ploughshares, and their spears into pruning hooks: nation shall not lift up sword against nation, neither shall they learn war any more" (Isa 2.1-5).

The prophet's inspired words, geographically and physically detailed, are not susceptible to easy twisting. He writes specifically 'concerning Judah and Jerusalem' (the people and the place) in 'the last days' (the time), when Jerusalem ('Zion') will become the earth's worship centre, disseminating God's law for the government of the whole planet. And the Lord Himself will be present, judging the Gentiles and establishing universal peace. To allegorize this (and it has to be allegorized as by no stretch of the imagination is its scenario of global prosperity evident today) into a prediction of the spread of the gospel is to do violence to language. And there is no need. Plainly and repeatedly the Old Testament foretells a period when the nation of Israel will be regathered to its land and spiritually restored to become the administrative centre of Messiah's kingdom (Jer 23.5-6; 31.31-40; Zech 14). Nor does the New Testament abrogate these promises. Read, for example, Matthew 19.28; Acts 3.19-21; Romans 11.25-29. The Bible is not a book of coded messages but a document to be read (in one sense at least) just like any other book: that is, "if the plain sense makes common sense seek no other sense lest it result in nonsense".

Perhaps a good place to start is 1 Corinthians 10.32 where Paul (describing the situation in Corinth, to be sure) says, "Give none offence, neither to the Jews, nor to the Gentiles, nor to the church of God". In that city there were three distinct groupings of people: the Jews (who met in the synagogue), Gentiles (who consorted in the various pagan temples) and the local assembly (separate from both). We can, I think, legitimately extrapolate from that a broad division of humanity. After all, Genesis chapters 1 to 11 are about mankind in general, but after chapter 12 God calls out one man to become the founding father of a nation which takes its name from his grandson Jacob. And Israel was set apart from all others as an oasis of godliness in a pagan world. It forms the great subject of most of the Old Testament. But the New Testament introduces us to the Lord Jesus, Israel's Messiah, rejected by His own people (John 1.11-12) but gladly received by others. Knowing His rejection by the nation, He announced the formation of an altogether new company, one He called "my church" (Matt 16.18), a company which, as the New Testament shows, consists of saved Jews *and* Gentiles (Acts 11.17-18; 15.14; Gal 3.28). We thus have three groups: (i) Gentiles (all the world apart from the Jewish nation), (ii) Israel (a nation formed by God for God, and given a land, a law, and a liturgy – if you'll pardon the alliteration, but I'm trying to précis Paul's words in Romans 9.4-5), and (iii) the church . Now the church is a unique company of spiritually saved individuals called out – for the Greek word *ekklesia* suggests exactly that – from all nations to be so intimately linked with Christ as to constitute metaphorically His body (Eph 1.22-23), His building (Eph 2.19-22), His bride (Eph 5.22-33).

What are the differences? First, their **beginnings**. Israel can trace its inception to the call of Abraham and the exodus from Egypt, by which time Jacob's family of 70 had become a nation. The church, on the other hand, was brought into existence by Spirit baptism which took place historically on the Day of Pentecost (1 Cor 12.13; Acts 1.5; 2.1-4; 11.15-16). Second, their **membership**. Although Israel was nationally redeemed from slavery, not every individual Israelite was spiritually saved, for "they are not all Israel [genuinely in the good of a relationship with God such as Jacob enjoyed], which are of Israel [merely physically descended from Jacob]" (Rom 9.6). Most of the chosen nation remained unregenerate. When Elijah complained that he was the only believer left God responded, "I have reserved to myself seven thousand men, who have not bowed the knee to *the image of* Baal". In other words, there was an election (genuinely saved people) within an election (a nation chosen to earthly privilege). Old Testament Israel therefore consisted of saved and unsaved. Says Paul, "at this present time also there is a remnant according to the election of grace" (Rom 11.5), because genuinely saved Israelites today are in the church the body of Christ. But – and here's the point – within the body of Christ (to be distinguished from a local assembly where it is possible for fakes to creep in) are no unbelievers: the church is a company of saved folk. Third, their **hope**. The earthly nation descended physically from Abraham through Isaac and Jacob had its hopes focused upon the land God had given it (Gen 12.1-3; 13.14-17; 15.18-21). Blessing was tied to that land; for though the gift was unconditional and irrevocable, the occupation of it was dependent upon obedience. Obedience ensured happy prosperity (Deut 28.1-14), but disobedience guaranteed removal and captivity (Deut 28.15-68). The church, by contrast, is a heavenly people (Phil 3.20-21), looking always for the coming of its Lord to take it home to glory (1 Thess 1.9-10). Fourth, their **worship**. Israel was divided into warriors (the men of military age), workers (Levites who carried the tabernacle furniture) and worshippers (the priests, Aaron's family, granted the privilege of superintending the nation's sacrifices). Believers today, however, are all three at once – that is, we are all, by God's grace, intended to engage in spiritual warfare (Eph 6.1-10), serve as the Lord directs us (Rom 12.4-8), and offer worship as a holy and royal priesthood (1 Pet 2.5,9).

One of the dangers of replacement theology is that it encourages the importing of Jewish temple ideas into the church: hence a separate priesthood with special regalia, incense, altars, ornate rituals, consecrated buildings, and the like. One only has to look at the interior of an Anglican Church to see the deleterious effects of this. But New Testament believers worship simply "in spirit and in truth" (John 4.24), our thoughts centred upon an invisible Saviour in glory rather than on the external trappings of a "worldly sanctuary" (Heb 9.1). That is why we need no special building; to remember the Saviour all that is required is bread and wine. There are other differences (for example, Israel's key day was the Sabbath; ours is the first of the week), but these should suffice. Lesson: properly to understand the purpose of God and the word of God we must avoid confusing Israel and the church. May the Lord help you as you feast on His truth.

Affectionately as always in Christ Jesus

WEEK FORTY FIVE

Letter No 45:

Speaking in Tongues

Since we are currently going through 1 Corinthians on Sunday evenings it seems appropriate to write to you about an issue you are bound to encounter sooner or later. So here is advance warning! One day you will bump into people, often genuine believers in the Lord Jesus, usually fresh, enthusiastic and plausible, who will tell you that their spiritual life was revolutionised when they began to speak in tongues. Occasionally they come from the old Pentecostal denominations (Elim or Assemblies of God), but more likely they attend one of the many newer charismatic companies. They will urge you to get the experience yourself, subtly hinting that your Christianity is seriously lacking if you miss out on it. How should we respond to such pressure? Certainly, were there a sure-fire biblical recipe for spiritual victory it would be both foolish and dishonouring to God to disregard it. On the other hand, we are not to read the Bible by experiences, our own or other people's; rather, we judge experiences by the word. I can think back to a time years ago when a young man accused me of blasphemy against the Holy Spirit because I had dared to suggest that the practices in which he found such comfort should be assessed in the light of scripture.

The first thing to bear in mind is that not all spiritual gifts listed in the New Testament are still functioning. And this is no groundless assumption – it is clearly taught in the word itself. For a start, it should be plain that there are no apostles now. Consider their distinctive features. They were personally chosen by the Lord Jesus (Mark 3.13-15) to act as His resurrection witnesses (Acts 1.22; 4.33) and to complete the revelation of the scriptures (John 16.13-15; 2 Peter 3.2), their exclusive position supported by the ability to work outstanding credential miracles, miracles which set them apart from other believers (2 Cor 12.12; Acts 2.43; 5.12).

The Lord selected only twelve during His earthly ministry. After His ascension the remaining eleven chose Matthias to replace Judas; and it would appear even in those early days they could find only two men who fulfilled the requirements of having "companied with us all the time that the Lord Jesus went in and out among us, beginning from the baptism of John, unto that same day that he was taken up from us" (Acts 1.21-22). But the Lord Himself later intervened from heaven to call Saul (Gal 1.1; Acts 9.3-6), who goes on to refer to himself as the final witness of the resurrection (1 Cor 15.8-9): "last of all he was seen of me also". The apostolate is therefore definitively closed, despite all the arguments of Roman Catholicism in favour of "apostolic succession" or the claims of cults like Mormonism. And along with apostles go New Testament prophets (1 Cor 12.28; Eph 3.5; 4.11). Prophecy in the New Testament, you see, is essentially no different from prophecy in the Old: that is, God revealed Himself directly through chosen instruments, disclosing truth hitherto hidden. It is not to be confused with teaching, for teaching opens up what God has already revealed in the written word, while prophecy communicates new unscripturated truth. Peter's description of Jewish prophecy therefore applies equally to the early days of the church: "prophecy came not in old time by the will of man: but holy men of God spake *as they were* moved by the Holy Ghost" (2 Pet 1.21). Paul speaks of the church as built upon "the foundation of the apostles and prophets" (Eph 2.20); both gifts were locked into the brief foundation stage of the church, that period when believers were reliant on special oral revelations before the canon of scripture was complete. But a building is not purely foundation – upon that rises the superstructure, resting on the foundation but not enlarging it. Thus we have no need of apostles (or prophets) today because we have "the apostles' doctrine" (Acts 2.42) in the complete word of God. Even in New Testament times there were fakes (Rev 2.2; 1 John 4.1). So beware of anyone who claims to be an apostle or a prophet. You can be certain he isn't and that he is dangerous.

All this leads us to the business of tongues. Let's ask three questions. First, **where do they appear in scripture?** To hear some charismatic friends speak one would imagine that tongues speaking was a mainstream biblical phenomenon. But what are the facts? It is mentioned only once in the gospels in a passage predicting the future miraculous manifestations which would validate the apostles' message (Mark 16.17-18). It then turns up thrice in the Acts, but each occasion is an unrepeatable event (Acts 2.1-11; 10.44-48; 19.1-7). The first is the birthday of the church; the second marks the first time Gentiles are brought into the church on an equal footing with converted Jews; the third involves twelve disciples of John Baptist who had become caught in a dispensational time warp and needed to be brought into full Christian blessing. Each case stands alone and cannot be paralleled today. Finally, the only letter to mention tongues speaking is 1 Corinthians, addressed not insignificantly to what might well be the most carnal and disorderly assembly in the New Testament. At the least it is self-evident that tongues speaking is no guarantee of spirituality. Although spiritual gifts are mentioned in later letters like Romans 12.3-8; Ephesians 4.11-12; 1 Peter 4.10-11 the subject of tongues is never again raised.

Second, **what were tongues?** Modern practitioners normally claim to be uttering ecstatic speech (glossolalia is the technical term) or angelic languages (from a misunderstanding of Paul's hyperbole in 1 Corinthians 13.1). But the biblical evidence is remarkably consistent. The first historical occurrence of this spiritual gift (and therefore the definitive description) is on the day of Pentecost when ordinary Galilean disciples suddenly and spontaneously began to speak intelligibly in genuine human languages which they had never learned. Although the local Hebrew-speaking inhabitants of Jerusalem could not make sense of what they heard and therefore scornfully accused the disciples of drunkenness, God had arranged that Jews from various parts of the Roman Empire visiting Israel for the feast were on site to validate the miracle (Acts 2.1-13). Remember that this was an exceptional moment in history: the Spirit of God came, in accordance with the Lord's promise, to form the body of Christ and indwell all believers individually. One of the startling miracles accompanying the unique descent of the Holy Spirit was not meaningless babble but coherent speech. After all, mere gobbledegook has been and still is the practice of a variety of world religions. Indeed, the Corinthians may well have engaged in it in their pre-conversion pagan days (1 Cor 12.2). But our God specialises in the genuinely and fittingly miraculous. Now this event is the touchstone for all biblical tongues-speaking. Because exactly the same terminology is used to describe the phenomenon in Paul's letter to the Corinthians, we can be sure there was no qualitative difference between what happed at Pentecost and what some Corinthians were doing. The KJV translators insert "unknown" before "tongue" in 1 Corinthians 14 not to suggest that the languages were unearthly but to indicate that they had not been made known to their speakers through the usual route of human instruction.

Third – and this is the key question – **why were tongues given?** "With *men of* other tongues and other lips will I speak unto this people; and yet for all that will they not hear me, saith the Lord. Wherefore tongues are for a sign, not to them that believe, but to them that believe not" (1 Cor

14.21-22). Paul quotes Isaiah 28.11-12 where judgment was predicted on the rebellious northern kingdom of Israel, which had rejected earlier appeals by God's prophets. The arrival of foreign troops speaking a strange tongue (the Assyrians in 2 Kings 17.22,23) would signal divine displeasure. In fact, Israel had long been forewarned of this token of judgment (Deut 28.49-51; Isa 33.19; Jer 5.15,19). Historically Israel was dispersed by the Assyrians in 722 BC, Judah by the Babylonians in 586 BC, and the Jews because of their rejection of Messiah in AD 70 (by the Romans, Luke 19.41-44). "This people" therefore means Israel not Gentiles; "other tongues" refers to genuine human languages not infantile babble; and 'they will not hear me' indicates that the sign was not of grace but rather a sealing of the nation's impenitence. The conclusion? Tongues were a sign, not primarily for the benefit of Christians, but for unbelieving Israelites. Their function was not to edify saints but to announce judgment. In other words, they were not intended for use in the local assembly at all, hence Paul's downgrading of them in his letter. The Corinthians were in error even in those days; and nobody is speaking in real biblical tongues today for the gift's function has terminated. All efforts to simulate tongues are therefore dangerously self-deluding. So let us make sure we never paddle up experience-centred backwaters but rather concentrate on those wonderful 'spiritual blessings in heavenly *places* in Christ' which are the birthright of all saints. Keep going!

Affectionately as ever in Christ Jesus

Letter No 46:

Politics

Since the prolonged overture to a forthcoming American presidential election has been playing loudly in the news over the past weeks, I thought I'd jot down a few thoughts about the thorny question of the believer's relationship to politics. You will probably already have discovered that among Christians there is a quite a range of views. For example, the very influential Fundamentalist lobby in the USA strongly advocates active involvement in the political process as the duty of a Christian citizen. Others go further and seek to draw God's people into the political arena through demonstrations, strikes, and social action. There is even a vocal group (called Dominionists or Reconstructionists) who believe that it is their vocation to place the whole of society under Old Testament Mosaic Law.

Of course, universal suffrage was not an issue in Bible times and is therefore not considered directly. Israel was a theocratic nation; other people had a variety of governmental forms, but none was a democracy in the modern sense. Nevertheless, where scripture does not rule directly, it always offers guiding principles which we disregard to our loss.

The first principle is to get **the right perspective** on the whole business of human government. Only the child of God is really aware of what is going on in this world, and that not because he reads his daily paper but because he listens to God's word. The foundation truth is that "power belongeth unto God" (Psa 62.11). No matter what political upheavals shake the nations nothing can alter the reality of ultimate divine power. But not only does scripture assert the sovereign rule of God in the affairs of men, it further teaches that He has seen fit to put delegated power into their hands in order to curb evil in a fallen world. God has ordained human government (Gen 9.1-6), He removes and sets up individual rulers (Dan 4.17,34-5), and even uses overtly ungodly men to fulfil His purpose (Rev 17.17). We are therefore compelled to conclude that, while governments may not always act as God prescribes in His word, in the final analysis all act as He permits. And the Christian's responsibility is plain: practical submission is commanded for all believers to all forms of government, be they good or bad (Rom 13.1-7). This requires, for example, that we respect and obey both police and traffic wardens for the sufficient reason that they are "ordained of God".

A second point is to consider **the Christian's position**. Old Testament Israel was a nation under God with a land, a temple, and instructions to function as the instrument of divine judgement in a godless world. But there are no theocratic governments today, and will never be until the Lord comes back to reign. The New Testament believer is a heavenly citizen, a stranger and pilgrim as far as the earth is concerned, and called to act as an ambassador for Christ (Phil 3.20-21; 1 Pet 2.11-12). Only a failure to appreciate such precious privileges will encourage the believer to become enmeshed in the politics of a world to which he no longer belongs.

Third, we should remember **the Christian's purpose.** Contrary to popular belief the child of God has not been left on earth to improve it or "bring in the kingdom". Scripture gives us no warrant to expect the former, nor any mandate to attempt the latter, which is the exclusive prerogative of the Lord Jesus Christ at His return in glory (Rev 19.11-21). Why then are we here? The New Testament answer is clear enough (Matt 28.18-20; Acts 1.8). Not to better society (after all, Christians have been around for nearly two millennia and godliness is hardly on the increase), not to set up what some call a "Christian counter culture", not to clean up the environment, but to preach the gospel and live for Christ. In His sovereign mercy, God is currently engaged in a glorious salvage operation: snatching men and women from a hell-bent civilisation into a saving relationship with Himself through the finished work of Christ on Calvary. This being so, politics at best are an irrelevance for the child of God, at worst a dangerous distraction from his God-given task of evangelism and holy living. We must beware of anything which constitutes an unequal yoke or an entanglement, for no political party has room for Christ. You only have to listen to the rival party contestants in the USA to see how much is based upon

Hollywood style glamour, money, self-promotion and false promises. As one Bible teacher wrote years ago, "trying to save the world by socialism [or conservatism, or liberalism, or Scottish Nationalism] is like cleaning and decorating the state rooms of a sinking ship". We just do not have the time to waste.

Fourth, we should follow **the pattern of godly men**. Our greatest example is the Lord Jesus Himself (John 17.18). He, Israel's rightful king, submitted Himself to the rule of the occupying Romans, refused to advocate resistance of any kind, suffered wrongful arrest, and thus stands as the supreme model of patient endurance (1 Pet 2.23). New Testament believers followed the trail He blazed. Paul avoided involvement with matters political when he bore the gospel around the Mediterranean world (1 Cor 2.2), and the early disciples in Jerusalem, despite their numerical strength, never attempted to remove the ruling Jewish party or the Roman overlords. When persecution came, which it did, instead of parading they prayed. Spiritual people fight only with spiritual weapons (2 Cor 10.4).

Fifth, it is wise to bear in mind **the Christian's prospect**. Our God, who controls all things, has a strategy in His programme of redemption. "It is striking", writes another, "that present salvation is mentioned in scripture exclusively in terms of spiritual blessings. Thus present salvation has nothing to do with economic, material, or social matters. The socio-political element of salvation is reserved for the future". We can therefore rejoice in the unshakeable purpose of God for this poor world – our Saviour is coming back to reign! Then, and only then, will the whole vexed business of politics, justice, and human rights be dealt with, for the Righteous One will be on the throne (Isa 32.1; Jer 23.5).

So we know what lies ahead. But how does all this affect our outlook now? It gives us strength to endure injustice and wrong, knowing that God will put all straight in His own good time (Jas 5.7-11). By now the biblical picture should be coming clear to you. It is summed up in the simple but costly word, *submission*. This means that we pray for the government (whoever resides in Downing Street), pay our taxes, and obey the authorities (1 Tim 2.1-3; Rom 13.6; 1 Pet 2.13-19). The only exception is when obedience would involve contradicting a plain scripture (Acts 4.18-20). But even then the apostles submitted unresistingly to the penalty of the law, "rejoicing that they were counted worthy to suffer shame for his name". Of course, we shall immediately be accused of opting out and failing to exercise an influence for good in a sick world. But far from such separation from politics producing a lack of impact, the opposite seems to be the case. Abraham outside had a greater influence on the fate of Sodom than Lot who dwelt within (Gen 18,19). Like Abraham, then, let us remain outside the snares of this world so that we may devote our energies fully to the glorious service of our soon coming Lord. And when He reigns all will be well!

Affectionately as ever in Christ Jesus

Letter No 47:

The Pilgrim's Progress (vi)

Time, I think, for yet another thrilling instalment of *The Pilgrim's Progress*. Today I want to do something different and introduce you to a whole family, just to show how apparently innocuous ideas may all too easily develop into serious departure from the faith.

The parents of this thriving family are **Mr and Mrs Love Is Everything**. In other words, their great emphasis is upon love at all costs. Why become obsessed to the point of disagreement over the finicky details of various minor doctrines when the main thing is to manifest the love of Christ? And let's face it, there is much to be said for their point of view. After all, does not Paul say in 1 Corinthians 13.1-3 that the highest service without love is of no value?

> "Though I speak with the tongues of men and of angels, and have not charity, I am become *as* sounding brass, or a tinkling cymbal. And though I have *the gift of* prophecy, and understand all mysteries, and all knowledge; and though I have all faith, so that I could remove mountains, and have not charity, I am nothing. And though I bestow all my goods to feed *the poor*, and though I give my body to be burned, and have not charity, it profiteth me nothing".

Trouble is, some folk who speak the loudest about love seem to have a hidden agenda. I remember many years ago taking part in a conference where an opportunity was given for written questions from the floor and up came the old chestnut about the oral participation of women in the meetings of the local church. It soon became clear that my platform colleague and myself held opposing views on this subject. After I had tried, doubtless very ineptly, to point out from 1 Corinthians 14.34-38 and 1 Timothy 2.8-12 what I believed the biblical teaching was, the other speaker commented that this might be so, but of course what really mattered in the Christian life was love. This seemed to be a way of parachuting out from the tiresomeness of grappling seriously with what scripture says, almost hinting that anyone who disagreed was guilty of being unloving. But love does not foreclose concern over doctrinal matters. It is not at odds with truth. Love is indeed vital, but we need to be clear exactly what scriptural love is. In this context of course it is not human sexual attraction, but neither is it that wishy-washy sentimentality which tolerates anything regardless of God's revealed truth. The first duty of love, you see, is toward God Himself. This is solid Old Testament teaching, fully endorsed by the Lord Jesus in the New: "thou shalt love the LORD thy God with all thine heart, and with all thy soul, and with all thy might" (Deut 6.5; Matt 22.36-40). The same chapter of 1 Corinthians which so memorably describes love in action notes that it "rejoiceth not in iniquity, but rejoiceth in the truth" (v.6). There is therefore no conflict between biblical love and biblical truth. In fact the Lord Jesus told His disciples in the plainest terms imaginable how they were to display their love for Him. "If ye love me, keep my commandments. . .he that hath my commandments, and keepeth them, he it is that loveth me: and he that loveth me shall be loved of my Father, and I will love him, and will manifest myself to him" (John 14.15,21). And again: "If a man love me, he will keep my words: and my Father will love him, and we will come unto him, and make our abode with him. He that loveth me not keepeth not my sayings" (14.23-24). And again: "Ye are my friends, if ye do whatsoever I command you" (15.14). That is to say, genuine love for the Saviour will manifest itself in scrupulous obedience to His commands; and 2 Peter 3.2 reminds us that the written teachings of the apostles constitute His commands just as much as His recorded words in the gospels. Do I love the Lord Jesus? The Jews were taught that love for Jehovah would be seen in practical submission to His commandments (Exod 20.6; Deut 11.1; 30.16; Josh 22.5; Dan 9.4). Likewise, the test of my devotion is not lip service, nor how many hymns of lusty loyalty I may sing but how far I endeavour to put into practice His word. All of which uncompromisingly demands that I read and seek to understand the scriptures. The mantra of love may merely be a convenient cop-out from the hard work of Bible study.

Now in the mercy of God Mr and Mrs Love Is Everything may have inherited from an earlier, more faithful generation a residual if unconscious habit of biblical obedience so that they personally are preserved from outright departure. But their offspring (and let us assume their union has been blessed with issue – as Thurber puts it in one of his lovely cartoons) may be of a different mind. Let us grant them two children: Master Doctrine Doesn't Matter, and his sister little Miss Feel Good Factor. Once we exalt love as the grace which trumps truth we are in danger of downgrading doctrine altogether. **Master Doctrine Doesn't Matter,** nurtured on a diet of smiling indifference, will mature into a manhood in which the teaching of the Bible is just one of many viable alternatives. And where there is no authoritative word from heaven we are left with nothing but human preferences, when every man does "what is right in his own eyes" (Deut 12.8; Judges 21.25). After all, if doctrine is trivial, why bother to read the word at all?

Little Miss Feel Good Factor takes this subjectivism a stage further by unashamedly exalting her feelings over the propositional truths taught in the word. A lady came up to me years ago (nothing seems to happen to me in the present, you notice!) to say that although she could see that the New Testament was opposed to the practice of splitting up a local church into house groups she personally found them very fulfilling and would therefore continue with them. And so personal gratification takes precedence over the word. You may remember that it is Ignorance in the real *Pilgrim's Progress* whose stock answer, when challenged about spiritual matters, is "My heart tells me so". Christian's response is pointed: "Thy heart tells thee so! Except the word of God beareth witness in this matter, other testimony is of no value". Yes, "the heart is deceitful above all things" and cannot be trusted as a guide, even after conversion. And if our feelings are untrustworthy, so too is the pragmatism which says "If it works it must be right". Once the Bible is displaced as the absolute authority anything can take its place – personal feelings, marketing techniques, the popular consensus, the latest fashions. No: for the believer, if it is right (that is, if it is according to the word) it will work, although the evidence of success may await eternity. God looks to the long-term. Paul told Timothy of a time when men "shall turn away *their* ears from the truth, and shall be turned unto fables [*muthos*, which gives us our 'myth']" (2 Tim 4.4). From truth to fables: as G K Chesterton put it, "when men cease to believe in God they do not believe in nothing, they believe in anything". If, as is all too likely, Miss Feel Good Factor grows up and marries **Mr No Convictions At All**, their child will probably be **Master Scoffing Unbelief,** trained from infancy to laugh at his grandparents' values (2 Pet 3.3).

The great lesson (and the reliable safeguard) for us is to rest on the word of God *and nothing else*. There alone we find what to believe and how to behave as those upon whom the Living God has showered His love in

Christ Jesus "while we were yet sinners". And our love for Him will be seen in our obedient loyalty to what He commands. May the Lord therefore grant us grace to seek to do what is right in His sight, not because it makes us feel good or attracts popular approval or even because it works, but simply because it is right.

Affectionately as ever in Christ Jesus

Letter No 48:

The God of Order

Our visiting speaker on Saturday night told us that the God who expects all things to be done "decently and in order" in our assembly gatherings (1 Cor 14.40) exemplifies this in His own written word. And certainly there is a wonderful symmetry and design in the scriptures, a design which becomes all the more evident as we study it in detail. Like you I have been reading through the perennially exciting Book of the Acts, a book packed with some of the greatest adventure stories in the New Testament. It traces the footsteps of the apostles as they discharge their task of carrying the gospel of the Lord Jesus into a hostile world, starting from Jerusalem and reaching out to Rome.

I was particularly taken by Peter's words to the Sanhedrin (Acts 5.29-32), which seem to me to be arranged in a kind of chiastic pattern, thus:

We ought to obey God rather than men. (A1)
    The God of our fathers raised up Jesus, (B1)
        whom ye slew and hanged on a tree. (C1)
    Him hath God exalted with his right hand *to be* a Prince and a Saviour, (B2)
        for to give repentance to Israel, and forgiveness of sins. (C2)
    And we are his witnesses of these things; (B3)
and *so is* also the Holy Ghost, whom God hath given to them that obey him. (A2)

This structure highlights the relationship between the apostle's points. For example, element A brings together **the object and the outcome of Christian obedience.** Our duty is first of all to God rather than to men, Peter's words solemnly reminding us that in a fallen world this is likely to cause hostility and misunderstanding. And this was no mere theorising. A very real threat from the religious authorities was hanging over the apostles even as he spoke. Of course we must bend over backwards to avoid breaking the law (1 Pet 2.13) or giving offence (Matt 17.27), but when it comes to the crunch God takes precedence (Dan 3.16-18). Yet by way of encouragement we are reminded of the benefits of putting God first: when we initially obeyed the gospel we received the gift of the indwelling Holy Spirit, and therefore by God's grace we already possess sufficient inner strength to stand for Him.

Element B focuses upon **the great truth of the resurrection**. Peter does not follow the expected chronological order: instead of speaking about the Lord being slain by men and then raised by God he reverses it. Why? Well, this has the effect of foregrounding the resurrection fact as the divine overthrow of men's verdict upon the person and work of Christ. Peter therefore notes the historical event (B1), the exaltation (B2) and the evidence (B3). Christ's resurrection was the work of the God of Israel (the phrase "the God of our fathers" clearly ties up the apostolic message with the promises given to Abraham, Isaac and Jacob); more than a mere restoration to life it involved a glorification of Christ as Prince (the word means author, originator, leader, ruler) and Saviour, titles which emphasise His future role as Israel's king and deliverer. Further, God has provided unimpeachable proof of His Son's exaltation in the consistent eyewitness testimony of the apostles and the Holy Spirit Himself (backing their word with miraculous signs and working conviction in the hearts of men).

Element C concerns **Israel**, contrasting (C1) the nation's past crime (in rejecting and killing its Messiah, treating Him as the object of a divine curse – see the background in Deuteronomy 21.23 and Galatians 3.13) with its future conversion (C2) when God will grant it repentance and forgiveness. It is God who grants both the repentance and the pardon, in accordance with the prophecy of Zechariah: "And I will pour upon the house of David, and upon the inhabitants of Jerusalem, the spirit of grace and of supplications: and they shall look upon me whom they have pierced . . . In that day there shall be a fountain opened to the house of David and to the inhabitants of Jerusalem for sin and for uncleanness" (Zech 12.10; 13.1). Our God always takes the initiative. The same nation who pierced Messiah (here revealed as a divine person) will have its heart changed by an act of grace so that a future generation of Jews will turn to Him in repentance and faith, resulting in their cleansing from sin.

You might also notice that Peter's brief message has something to say about each person of the Trinity. God (in context, the Father) has raised and exalted the Lord Jesus; the Lord Jesus, though abused by men has been elevated by God with a view to His future office of ruler and rescuer of Israel (Zechariah 14.1-4 sets that coming scene); and the Holy Spirit, given by the Father to all who surrender to Christ, is witness to God's satisfaction with His Son. How marvellous that the entire Godhead has acted in grace towards sinners like us!

Now the sort of structural pattern I have noted in this short passage is not uncommon in scripture. On a larger scale you might consider the first chapter of Genesis where we read about the six days of God's creative activity. This is what someone has called the 'floodlight account' of creation, because it puts the making of man in its wider context. The spotlight account in Genesis 2, on the other hand, focuses upon the work of day 6, climaxing in a very detailed record of the formation of Adam and Eve. The clue to the arrangement in Genesis 1 is given in verse two: "And the earth was (i) without form, and (ii) void". The first word means unformed, the second unfilled. There follows the six days' work. In the first three days (Gen 1.3-13) the earth is formed in the sense of shaped and prepared for its inhabitants; in days four to six (Gen 1.14-31) it is filled with life. There seems therefore to be a broad parallel along the following lines:

The Work of Forming	The Work of Filling
Day 1: Light (vv.3-5)	Day 4: Light-bearers (sun, moon, stars) (vv.14-19)
Day 2: Firmament (space) (vv.6-8)	Day 5: Sea-life and birds (vv.20-23)
Day 3: Land, sea, plants (vv.9-13)	Day 6: Land-life, Man (vv.24-31)

Now, when I call this an arrangement I do not mean to give the impression that Genesis 1 is an example of poetic license detached from historical truth. On the contrary, I am saying that the wonderfully orderly God of the Bible actually did His creative work in this organized and methodical way, recording it accurately in His word for our learning.

Yes, as our speaker said yesterday, such a God of order rightly expects orderliness in His people. In his classic text *Spiritual Depression* D Martyn Lloyd-Jones writes, concerning the lowness of spirits some of us go through all too often, "the real trouble is an absence of discipline and order in their life". He is correct. If we seek by grace to discipline and order our lives according to the word we shall always have much to do, much to enjoy, much to be thankful for. And as a result we shall have no time to feel sorry for ourselves! May ours be lives ordered by and for God.

Affectionately as ever in Christ Jesus

WEEK FORTY NINE

Letter No 49:

The World, the Flesh and the Devil

You asked for a letter about the devil. Well, we must first line up and identify our three great spiritual adversaries:

> "And you *hath he quickened*, who were dead in trespasses and sins; Wherein in time past ye walked according to the course of this world [that is, the world system], according to the prince of the power of the air, the spirit that now worketh in the children of disobedience [the devil]: Among whom also we all had our conversation in times past in the lusts of our flesh [the sinful, flesh nature within us], fulfilling the desires of the flesh and of the mind; and were by nature the children of wrath, even as others" (Ephesians 2.1-3).

You have doubtless already noticed how scrupulously honest the Bible is about the real difficulties the believer will face in his life down here. Scripture could never be charged with infringing the trades' descriptions act. On the contrary, it forewarns us of serious trials and temptations (John 16.33). Around us is a hostile world system dominated by anti-God values (1 John 2.15-17), inside us is a reservoir of wickedness called the flesh (Rom 7.18), and finally, as it were permeating the air we breathe, is Satan himself (Eph 2.2; 1 Pet 5.8). The first foe has been called "a gigantic organisation opposed to God and all who are born of God" (George Cutting), "a vast order and system that Satan has promoted, which conforms to his ideals, aims, and methods. It is civilisation now functioning apart from God" (L S Chafer). This explains why, once we trust Christ, we face antagonism from friends, family and workmates. The world puts pressure on us to conform (Rom 12.2). The second enemy is even more distressing. To face external trouble is one thing; to find it within is quite another, yet every believer knows from bitter experience that his worst antagonist lurks in his own heart, still "deceitful above all things and desperately wicked" (Jer 17.9) even after conversion. The word "flesh" is perhaps best understood if we spell it backwards and cut off the h. Yes, my biggest enemy is my self: self-interest, self-esteem, self-indulgence, self-obsession, self-love. As Shakespeare's Richard III says:

> What do I fear? myself? there's none else by:
> Richard loves Richard; that is, I am I.

Just as I is the central letter of the word sin, so self is the root of our iniquity. But finally there is Satan, a powerful being who aims to shake the faith of God's people.

Let me draw your attention to a few basic Bible truths about him. Consider the episode just before His betrayal where the Lord Jesus tells Peter about Satan's animosity:

> "Simon, Simon, behold, Satan hath desired *to have* you [all the disciples], that he may sift *you* as wheat: But I have prayed for thee [Peter individually], that thy faith fail not: and when thou art converted, strengthen thy brethren" (Luke 22.31-32).

Here we learn first about Satan's **reality**. The Saviour was not speaking vaguely about some impersonal power, some abstract principle of evil, but a real, personal being. The pronoun ("he") and the verbs ("desire", "sift") make that plain, as does the narrative of the Lord's encounter with Satan in the wilderness (Matthew 4). To doubt the reality of Satan is to impugn the testimony of the incarnate Son of God. It appears that Satan was one of God's angelic creations who wilfully rebelled and has ever since led a host of wicked invisible spirits in opposition to God's programme. His names and descriptions provide an insight into his **activity**. As "the devil [*diabolus*]", he is the slanderer, the false "accuser of our brethren" (Rev 12.10). Let us not do Satan's work for him by speaking ill of our brothers and sisters in Christ. As Satan (Matt 4.10), he is the adversary who opposes God's people. As "the tempter" (Matt 4.3), he aims to seduce men into sin. As the father of lies (John 8.44), he is the consummate untruth-teller whose word cannot be trusted. As a "murderer from the beginning" (John 8.44), he is the one who deliberately led Adam into the sin that brought death upon the entire human race. The Book of Revelation significantly calls him the "old serpent" (Rev 12.9) thus identifying him with the instrument of evil in Eden. As "the wicked one"

(Matt 13.19), he is morally opposed to God, "the Holy One". As "the god of this world" (2 Cor 4.4), he is the unseen, unrecognised presiding force influencing the attitudes of the entire world system around us. And he is varied in his methods. After all, he has had many years of experience in dealing with fallen human beings. He can rush upon us like a roaring lion seeking to terrify (1 Pet 5.8); or he can transform himself into "an angel of light" (2 Cor 11.14), promising apparent blessing. He attacked the infant church initially with brute force (Acts 5.40-41), and when that failed embarked upon fraud, stirring up discontent or manufacturing fake conversions (Acts 6.1; 8.9-24).

His **hostility** is summed up: "he hath desired to have you, that he may sift you as wheat". He longs to get hold of and damage believers. And his **strategy** is best illustrated in Genesis when we see him cunningly persuading Eve to distrust God's word. His first recorded statement in the Old Testament, "*Hath* God said?" (Gen 3.1), insinuates doubt as to God's reliability, and the same tactic is repeated when he challenges the Father's public announcement of Christ's sonship with a sneering "if": "*If* thou be the Son of God" (Matt 3.17; 4.3). Alas, because our fallen nature, the flesh, is in full sympathy with him Satan has a ready-made foothold in our souls. The Lord Jesus was of course completely different: "the prince of this world cometh, and hath nothing in me" (John 14.30). No one but the impeccable (that is, not able to sin) Son of God could speak like that. Nevertheless, in God's goodness, we do have in the word a sure resource against Satan's wiles. "The shield of faith", practical confidence in the written word (Eph 6.16), can quench his darts. Therefore the answer to satanic assault is to flee to scripture (Prov 18.10) and cling to its promises. When doubts besiege the heart never forget the biblical recipe: faith comes by hearing and hearing by the word of God (Rom 10.17). Insofar as I imbibe the word my feeble faith will grow and stand firm.

But there is even better news. The Saviour reveals Satan's **inferiority** to God. Now this is a fundamental truth: the world is not governed by two equal but opposing powers who are eternally battling it out. No, the Bible does not teach dualism. Our God is sovereign, supreme, all glorious and uniquely omnipotent. Did you notice that the Lord Jesus says "Satan hath desired [*exaiteomai*] to have you"? Thayer's lexicon defines the verb thus: "to ask or beg for one's self, to ask that one be given up to one from the power of another". So Satan has to ask permission before he can touch a child of God! Further, look at the stated purpose: "that he may sift *you* as wheat". Is Satan really in the beneficial business of sieving wheat to remove the chaff? Of course not. He cannot affect our salvation so he aims to destabilize us and imperil our testimony. But God overrules his evil intention so that good comes of it: we are actually blessed by a process of trial which casts us upon the Lord. That is to say, God uses Satan as a tool by which to toughen up His people. Peter failed (in that he denied the Master) but his faith didn't. He didn't throw in the towel. I am sure he clung onto the Lord's words: "when thou art converted, strengthen thy brethren". "When", not "if". And as a result of that sifting experience he became spiritually stronger because less self-reliant. Once we learn our weakness we are the more willing to hide in Christ. So take heart! Satan may be powerful, but his freedom is limited and his destiny fixed (Rom 16.20; Rev 20.10) because our God is in total control.

Affectionately as ever in Christ Jesus

Letter No 50:

Choosing a Life Partner

Today I thought I'd attempt a rather daring theme for a crabby old bachelor. My father used to say (with a twinkle in his eye, I think) that marriage was like a besieged city: "those who are outside want to get in, and those who are inside want to get out". Hardly original, I suspect, but his words do highlight the important fact that, like many other responsibilities in life, marriage requires solid commitment alongside a recognition that its course will not always run smooth. Although I have no practical experience of matrimony (save that, not to be undervalued, of the interested and occasionally amused spectator), I can at least pass on to you some of the things I have learned from the scriptures. And they put the whole matter in the correct perspective. It may not at present be at the top of your list of priorities, but one day mayhap it will. So, as Polonius says, "perpend".

Here are ten biblical truths about marriage. First, it is a **divine creatorial institution.** By that I mean it was not introduced in the New Testament but in the Old, right at the start of man's existence. When asked about divorce the Lord Jesus immediately went back to the inspired creation account in Genesis to establish fundamental principles: "Have ye not read, that he which made *them* at the beginning made them male and female, And said, For this cause shall a man leave father and mother, and shall cleave to his wife: and they twain shall be one flesh? Wherefore they are no more twain, but one flesh. What therefore God hath joined together, let not man put asunder" (Matt 19.4-6). It is not a convenient social custom but a divinely ordained relationship. If you wish to get a grasp of the biblical teaching you can do no better than reread very carefully the first two chapters of Genesis.

Second, it is designed, as the Lord graciously permits, to be **fruitful.** The first command to a wedded couple in scripture is in Genesis 1.27-8: "So

God created man in his *own* image, in the image of God created he him; male and female created he them. And God blessed them, and God said unto them, Be fruitful, and multiply, and replenish the earth". The Bible knows nothing of a merely companionable marriage which deliberately avoids reproduction; on the contrary, children are seen not as an unwanted intrusion or a nuisance but as a distinct divine blessing (Psa 127.3-5). Of course, it is ultimately God who shuts or opens the womb as it pleases Him (Gen 29.31; 1 Sam 1.5). I have known several godly couples who have not been blessed with the children they would have dearly loved. But here, as in so much else, we must bow to God's sovereignty. He alone knows what is best for us.

Third, it is **heterosexual.** Genesis could not be clearer. Adam awoke from his deep sleep to be confronted not with Steve but Eve. The Bible is startlingly up to date in its analysis of what might appear to be modern trends in deviance; but there is really nothing new under the sun. Sin is very old-fashioned. Reading his Bible on the train a friend of mine was challenged by some sniggering youths who asked him "Good book, is it? Got any sex in it?" Yes indeed – sodomy, gang rape, incest, polygamy, onanism – it is all there. The shameful face of human wickedness and its terrible consequences are candidly recorded in scripture.

Fourth, it is **monogamous.** When I speak on this topic (rarely, of course) I tend here to venture a little joke and say "Please note: monogamous, *not* monotonous". One wife (or, to be precise, one wife at a time) is sufficient for any man. Adam awoke to find Eve only, not Eve and Susan and Maisy and Bessie and Millicent stretched out in a winding queue through Eden. And yet you will have noticed the oddity that God tolerated polygamy in the Old Testament. This, like Israel's divorce laws, was permitted "for the hardness of your hearts" (Matt 19.8). But it was not God's original purpose, and even the Old Testament narrative makes clear its destructive fruits in family and personal life (rivalry, jealousy, violence).

Fifth, it is **beneficial.** "*It is* not good that the man should be alone; I will make him an help meet for him" (Gen 2.18). Marriage is not just a wonderful cure for our loneliness, guaranteeing that affectionate intimacy which we all crave; it is a package of positive benefits. A godly wife brings to her husband qualities that he lacks in himself, so that the two of them together can serve the Lord more effectively than they could apart (Acts 18.26; Rom 16.3; 1 Cor 16.19). You have only to ask a Christian couple (or even watch them in their home) to discover what I mean. I can look thankfully at some of my friends and rejoice that God in His goodness has given them just the partners they needed.

Sixth, it is a **life sentence**. "They shall be one flesh" (Gen 2.24), among other things, indicates that the married couple become like one organism, bonded together in a life which nothing but death can dissolve. As the Saviour puts it, "And they twain shall be one flesh: so then they are no more twain, but one flesh. What therefore God hath joined together, let not man put asunder" (Mark 10.8-9). God joins; only God can sever. This teaching is repeated in the rest of the New Testament: "For the woman which hath an husband is bound by the law to *her* husband so long as he liveth; but if the husband be dead, she is loosed from the law of *her* husband. So then if, while *her* husband liveth, she be married to another man, she shall be called an adulteress: but if her husband be dead, she is free from that law; so that she is no adulteress, though she be married to another man" (Rom 7.2-3). "The wife is bound by the law as long as her husband liveth; but if her husband be dead, she is at liberty to be married to whom she will; only in the Lord" (1 Cor 7.39). The context of the first passage is particularly interesting as Paul is not primarily dealing with marriage at all (which he is in 1 Corinthians 7). Nevertheless he assumes (and it is essential to his argument) its inviolability. God hates "putting away" (Mal 2.15-16). Divorce is therefore not an option for the child of God.

Seventh, it is to be **God-honouring**. For the believer marriage must be "in the Lord" (1 Cor 7.39), that is, in accordance with His will. This is more than simply making sure (in line with the unequal yoke instruction in 2 Corinthians 6.14-18) that we marry a fellow believer. No, we must marry the fellow believer of God's choice for us. Your wife is to be spiritual help and encouragement to you; you will therefore look for a girl who is spiritually like-minded, one whose life displays her love for the Saviour. Never forget Amos 3.3 or the description of the godly wife in Proverbs 31.10-31.

Eighth, it is an **orderly relationship**. The husband is to take the lead (Eph 5.23), acting as the primary bread-winner (Gen 3.17-19) while the wife's special duty is as guardian of the home, bringing up children for the Lord (1 Tim 2.13-15; Tit 2.5). This is established in the very way God created Adam and Eve (Adam formed first, then Eve out of him and for him; 1 Cor 11.8-9). C S Lewis's *Mere Christianity* has some interesting things to say about the necessity of hierarchy in a party of two.

Ninth, it is **spiritually illustrative**. Only in the New Testament do we learn that Adam and Eve were made so as to picture a greater truth – the eternal relationship between the Lord Jesus Christ and His church (Eph 5.22-33). In God's universe the physical illustrates the spiritual. Every marriage, however faintly and failingly, hints at a grander reality and makes us long for the Marriage Supper of the Lamb when the saints of God will be for ever united to the Saviour (Rev 19.6-9).

Tenth, it is what we might call **normal but not obligatory**. The Lord's words in Matthew 19.10-12 and Paul's in 1 Corinthians 7.1,7-9,32-33 indicate that in some cases marriage is not in God's sovereign purpose. Each of us has to seek the Lord's face in these matters and submit to His gracious will, whatever it may be. Speaking as a single man, I would honestly not wish my condition upon anyone; on the other hand, I would even less wish you to be married to the wrong person. The way to be safe is to 'trust in the LORD with all thine heart; and lean not unto thine own understanding. In all thy ways acknowledge him, and he shall direct thy paths' (Prov 3.5-6). May you go on to enjoy God's best for you.

Affectionately as always in Christ Jesus

WEEK FIFTY ONE

Letter No 51:

Money Matters

Don't worry – I am not embarking upon a new career as a financial adviser. But as the fiscal year draws to its close it might make sense to pass on a few simple thoughts about the believer and money. Some years back a Christian student confided in me that he had just come into a substantial inheritance, much of which he had spent thoughtlessly before coming across Isaiah 57.13 in his Bible reading. "Then", said he, "I realised that these material possessions were potentially ousting God from His rightful place in my life". Well, he was quite correct; money can mess us up. The vast array of material products money can buy (cars, houses, computers, media technology, music, clothes, books, food – we can easily select our pet favourites), and the rather more insidious respectability it promotes can effectively become idols. An idol, remember, is whatever replaces in the Living God in my affections.

The pursuit of earthly wealth is the goal of a world blinded to spiritual realities. But how bluntly the scripture addresses God's ancient people when they begin to turn from Him to worship the false gods of their neighbours: "When thou criest [for help], let thy companies [of idols] deliver thee; but the wind shall carry them all away; vanity shall take *them*: but he that putteth his trust in me shall possess the land, and shall inherit my holy mountain" (Isa 57.13). This of course is the fundamental problem with idols – they just do not work. The acid test of those objects in which we place our confidence is *reality*. Can the thing that means most in my life come to my rescue in the hour of need? Can it deliver me from the fear of death, the pull of temptation, the thirst for lasting satisfaction? To give anyone or anything the pre-eminence which properly belongs to "the living and true God" (1 Thess 1.9) is sheer folly as well as sin.

The lesson is as timely today as when Isaiah first delivered his message. After all, affluence is rampant in the western world, creating pressure on believers to get on and get more. We are all encouraged to join the rush for prosperity. As a consequence, the Lord Jesus, His word, and the local assembly in which He has placed us all begin to take second place. The direful results are all too obvious: believers with swollen wallets and shriveled souls. Now I am not saying that we should live like impoverished hermits. Scripture emphasizes the practical value of work and the responsibility of caring for our dependants – both of which involve money. But what we have to get straight is that for the believer (whose ultimate citizenship is in heaven) money is simply a means to an end. Here then are three basic principles.

First, **the believer's assets are primarily spiritual**. I am sure you have noticed in your Bible reading the radical difference between the concepts of wealth in the two testaments. Israel's blessings were associated largely with the land God gave them. Even a cursory reading of Deuteronomy 28 should make that plain. Not surprisingly, then, the final punishment for disobedience was exile from the land. While we must not devalue Israel's very real spiritual riches, the fact remains that the normal outward evidence of genuine godliness was material success. I have not forgotten the Book of Job or Psalms 37 and 73. But the general pattern seems clear: "All these blessings shall come on thee ... if thou shalt hearken unto the voice of the Lord thy God" (Deut 28.2). But come the New Testament and there is a change. The Lord Jesus directed His disciples' attention away from the earth to heaven, the believer's eternally secure treasure house (Matt 6.20). For us, the real sphere of wealth is now "in the heavenlies in Christ" (Eph 1.3, J N Darby's translation), for our riches are spiritual, bound up with a risen Saviour. There is therefore now no necessary correlation between spirituality and material prosperity, between obedience to the word and physical reward. Indeed, sometimes they are exactly opposite. In the words of Bacon, "Prosperity is the blessing of the Old Testament; adversity is the blessing of the New". As the Lord writes to the church at Smyrna, "I know thy works, and tribulation, and poverty, (but thou art rich)" (Rev 2.9). All this means we must maintain the right perspective. Society will judge your success by the number of objects you own, but God's word exhorts us to see beyond the temporal, and "beware of covetousness: for a man's life consisteth not in the abundance of the things which he possesseth" (Luke 12.15). Listen to a man who had little of this world's goods: "though our outward man perish, yet the inward *man* is renewed day by day. For our light affliction, which is but for a moment, worketh for us a far more exceeding *and* eternal weight of glory; While we look not at the things which are seen, but at the things which are not seen: for the things which are seen *are* temporal; but the things which are not seen *are* eternal" (2 Cor 4.16-18). Yes, "godliness with contentment is great gain" (1 Tim 6.6). Make that your motto and cultivate a modest life-style in this world.

Second, **materialism is not a disease confined to the wealthy.** Two popular errors should be avoided. Prosperity Theology (so-called) assumes that it is God's will for every believer to be materially rich and physically healthy. This shows a failure to grasp the difference between Israel and the Church as well as an ignorance of the divine strategy (for Romans 8.23 teaches that the redemption of the body awaits the Lord's return). The other extreme might be labeled Poverty Theology because it argues that wealth *per se* is wrong. But what says the scripture? "The love of money [not money itself] is the root of all evil: which while some coveted after, they have erred from the faith, and pierced themselves through with many sorrows" (1 Tim 6.10). Paul aims some of his sharpest warnings at those who itch to be rich (1 Tim 6.9). His instruction to the wealthy is worth careful reading for its judicious balance (1 Tim 6.17-19). This helps us to eschew oversimplification and judgmentalism. Poverty is not in itself unimpeachable evidence of piety any more than riches are proof of righteousness. The temptations of greed, envy, covetousness and materialism are faced by all believers whatever their financial status.

Third, **the privilege of being generous is not denied to the poor.** We must not fall into the trap of thinking that a man has to be rich before he can enjoy the blessedness of giving (Acts 20.35). Some of the most notable givers in the word were those who had little. The Lord praised a widow who gave a mere two mites (Luke 21.1-4). Paul rejoiced in the Macedonian saints who, though poor themselves, longed to contribute to the relief of penurious believers in Judea: "in a great trial of affliction the abundance of their joy and their deep poverty abounded unto the riches of their liberality. For to *their* power, I bear record, yea, and beyond *their* power *they were* willing of themselves; Praying us with much intreaty that we would receive the gift, and *take upon us* the fellowship of the ministering to the saints. And *this they did*, not as we hoped, but first gave their own selves to the Lord, and unto us by the will of God" (2 Cor 8.2-5). This demolishes the myth that believers have to seek well-paid jobs in order to support the Lord's work (as though our God were in need of funds!) What the Lord requires from us first of all is far costlier than mere money (Prov 23.26).

Instead of becoming entangled in the prosperity trap (neatly described as "too many people buying what they don't want with money they don't have to impress people they don't like") we should aim to use what God has graciously given us for His glory. The Lord's parable in Luke 16.1-13 is pertinent: "the very best thing we can do with our money is to spend it for the Lord; and then instead of being rust on our souls it will be treasure in heaven" (CHM). May the Lord give you help to do what is right before Him.

Affectionately as always in Christ Jesus

WEEK FIFTY TWO

Letter No 52:

Your First Spiritual Birthday

It must now be approaching one year from the time when God in His marvellous grace opened your eyes to the truth of the gospel and drew you to Himself for salvation in Christ Jesus. You are therefore just about one year old spiritually! Happy birthday!

I considered celebrating this signal occasion with balloons, whistles and jam tarts, but since you are rather a big boy for that sort of thing I decided instead to sum up some of the benefits you have enjoyed since conversion. In Exodus 40 we are told that the tabernacle was completed *almost exactly one year* after the Israelites came out from Egyptian slavery to be constituted God's own special people: "And it came to pass in the first month in the second year, on the first *day* of the month, *that* the tabernacle was reared up" (Exod 40.17).

What had happened to them during that past year? **First**, they had been redeemed from the judgment of God through the death of the Passover lamb. Indeed, the Passover event involved a radical alteration in their calendar so that for ever afterwards that day became their national birthday and its month marked their new year: "This month *shall be* unto you the beginning of months: it *shall be* the first month of the year to you" (Exod 12.2). In the same way, your conversion brought you into "newness of life". The shed blood of a spotless lamb had been daubed on the lintel and doorposts of Israelite homes, so that the destroying angel would not enter to eliminate their firstborn. The spiritual application is obvious: the slaughter of the lamb pictures the historical death of Christ as "the lamb of God" (John 1.29), but the smearing of its blood speaks of practical faith in His finished work. You see, although you were the object of God's love from eternity, you did not come into the good of the Saviour's death until

193

the moment you took your shelter beneath the blood, announcing that you believed what He accomplished at the cross was sufficient to satisfy all God's righteous demands against you as a guilty sinner. That is blessing number one.

But Israel was not protected from God's wrath merely to linger on in Egypt. Their **second** blessing was that they were brought out from slavery by a divine display of power climaxing at the Red Sea when the pursuing armies were overwhelmed, for ever separating God's redeemed people from their enemies. Likewise, you have become an object of God's active deliverance, not from His wrath alone, but from bondage to sin and Satan. After all, the Lord Jesus came to save His people not simply from the eternal punishment their sins deserve but from the daily dominion of sin itself (Matt 1.21; Rom 6.1-6).

But was Israel left to wander at will? No, for the God who delivered His people had the right to direct them. He therefore went before them in a pillar of cloud and fire (guidance 24/7!) to steer their steps through the desert to the Promised Land (Exo 13.21-22). This, their **third** blessing, typifies our guidebook, the written word of God which is "a lamp unto my feet, and a light unto my path" (Psa 119.105). How absurd to trust the Bible when it comes to the matter of eternal salvation and yet ignore its instructions as to daily life and worship down here! I am so glad that, early in your Christian life, you saw that the scripture leads you to baptism and the local assembly, and acted accordingly. And obedience can be costly – the religious world sneers at a small, simple company meeting in submission to the word. Of course, the Bible does not necessarily answer every question which may arise in our lives (what job to pursue, where to live, whom to marry) but it does establish clear principles of behaviour which we disregard to our peril (2 Tim 3.16-17). Israel had just to look up and follow the cloud; we have to read the word regularly and intelligently, prayerfully applying its lessons. That is the pattern for the rest of your life in this world.

A **fourth** stage in Israel's progress was their song of deliverance after the miracle of the Red Sea. For the first time they sang to express their joy at salvation:

> "Then sang Moses and the children of Israel this song unto the LORD, and spake, saying, I will sing unto the LORD, for he hath triumphed gloriously: the horse and his rider hath he thrown into the sea. The LORD *is* my strength and song, and he is become my salvation" (Exod 15.1-2).

The tune isn't recorded but the words are as a model of appropriate praise. God's people are saved from sin that they might render to Him the worship which is His due (John 4.23-24). I have listened with inexpressible delight as you have found your voice in prayer and praise. Do keep at it. Although the Lord may give you service to do for Him in days to come, I hope you will never forget that, as a member of a holy priesthood, your first function is to offer up adoration (1 Pet 2.5; Heb 13.15). It is all too easy to put platform ministry above our duty as worshippers. Hearts full of Christ will never be slow to express their appreciation of Him. That is why the breaking of bread meeting is so central.

But after that exhilarating song came trials: "they could not drink of the waters of Marah, for they *were* bitter: therefore the name of it was called Marah. And the people murmured" (Exod 15.23-24). Testing moments like this made Israel aware of the sinfulness of their own hearts because, despite redemption, they were always quick to blame God for any disappointment. And we are no different. Salvation does not eradicate the flesh nature; indeed, the ups and downs of the Christian pathway bring out from our hearts the sourness within. But Israel's **fifth** blessing was to discover that God was equal to every emergency. The tree that sweetened bitter water hints at Calvary (Exod 15.25; 1 Pet 2.24), the eternally indelible reminder of God's love for His own (Rom 5.8). All our circumstances, whether good or bad, are ordered by His hand, and He alone can transform sorrow into joy, giving us "songs in the night" (Job 35.10). You have not yet climbed Hill Difficulty, but when you reach its foothills, which you will, remember Israel's experience and cast yourself upon a faithful God.

Sixth, amidst a barren wilderness Israel was granted an unfailing supernatural food supply (Exod 16.35). Manna speaks of the Lord Jesus as the living bread of life who came from heaven (John 6.32). There is nothing in this sinful world to satisfy our new life, so we must feast daily upon His person in order to nourish our souls for the demands of the journey. Be daily occupied with Him (Exod 16.21) and your heart will be encouraged.

More – wonderful to tell – you are not alone on the journey. Israel's **seventh** blessing was to discover the power of the few on the mountain top upholding the many in battle below (Exod 17.10-11). The corporate prayer of faithful believers in the fellowship of the local assembly sustains us in our walk and service for God. I am sure you are coming to appreciate the value of older saints who cannot get out as they once used to but who nonetheless can mention you before the throne of grace. And you can do likewise for others. So many blessings! "Bless the LORD, O my soul, and forget not all his benefits: Who forgiveth all thine iniquities; who healeth all thy diseases; Who redeemeth thy life from destruction; who crowneth thee with lovingkindness and tender mercies; Who satisfieth thy mouth with good *things; so that* thy youth is renewed like the eagle's" (Psa 103.2-5). Always remember that though men may let you down your God and Father never will. And He who has kept you thus far will keep you to the end.

Affectionately as ever in Christ Jesus